*The
Football and Rugby
Team Nicknames
of Wales*

THE
FOOTBALL AND RUGBY
TEAM NICKNAMES
OF WALES

RICHARD E. HUWS

PAUL WATKINS
DONINGTON
2013

Published by

PAUL WATKINS
(an imprint of Shaun Tyas)
1 High Street
Donington
Lincolnshire
PE11 4TA

ISBN
978–1–907730–24–5

Printed and bound in Wales
by Gwasg Dinefwr Press, Llandybie, Carmarthenshire

CONTENTS

v

ABBREVIATIONS

AFC   Association Football Club
CPD   Clwb Pêl Droed [Football Club]
CR   Clwb Rygbi [Rugby Club]
DFC   Disability Football Club
DRFC Disability Rugby Football Club
FC   Football Club
LFC   Ladies' Football Club
LRFC Ladies' Rugby Football Club
RFC   Rugby Football Club
RLFC Rugby League Football Club

INTRODUCTION

In 2009 I compiled a volume entitled *The football and rugby playing fields of Wales* which was published by Y Lolfa, Talybont, Ceredigion. (ISBN 978-184771-145-8). During the course of my research into that volume I accumulated many references to team nicknames, some of which were included in the narrative. I found the background to many of those names quite fascinating, and when some further work revealed several hundred more examples this prompted me to consider the possibility of a companion volume. I was particularly fortunate to find, through mutual friends, John & Sheila Rowlands of Cardiff, that Dr Shaun Tyas of Donington, Lincolnshire was also working on a similar project, restricted to association football teams, but covering the whole of the British Isles in its scope. Not only did much of our research overlap, but Shaun was also a publisher who kindly offered to publish my work as a separate entity for which I am most grateful. Since we made that initial contact we have very happily collaborated and freely exchanged information, and I am very grateful to him for his very kind co-operation at all times which I am sure can only enrich both publications.

As noted, this work includes the football and rugby team nicknames of Wales, and in some instances, teams from the same town or village share the same nickname. I have also included the nicknames of both union and league rugby codes, together with disability and women's teams. It was often difficult to distinguish between nicknames and suffixes, and for the purpose of this study, both have been included. Wherever possible, comparisons have also been drawn with teams outside Wales and beyond who carry the same nickname or suffix, as this has often helped to explain the derivation and significance of the name. In most instances it has been possible to identify why a particular nickname arose, but this has not always been the case, and some will remain a mystery. I have, in many examples, tried to offer an explanation, but in some instances I may be incorrect in my assumptions.

1

As with *The football and rugby playing fields of Wales,* I am very grateful to numerous institutions and individuals for their assistance. Above all, I would like to thank my former colleagues at the National Library of Wales, Aberystwyth for their assistance. I am particularly grateful to Rhydian Davies, Jayne Day, Emyr Evans, Elen Owen, and Gwynant Phillips for their unfailing support; E. Aled Jones was particularly helpful and drew my attention to several names which I would otherwise have almost certainly ovelooked, and Gethin Williams provided invaluable help through his contacts in Anglesey. I would also like to express my warmest thanks to three eminent rugby historians – my good friend John M. Jenkins of Bow Street, Tony Lewis of Pyle, and Gwyn Prescott of Cardiff for identifying several rugby nicknames which were new to me and providing additional background information on their derivation. Their assistance is also much appreciated.

I am also grateful to many Welsh public libraries and archive offices (including the Royal Commission on Ancient & Historical Monuments of Wales) for their assistance, guidance and exemplary standard of service at all times. I also e-mailed many individual clubs and local authority representatives seeking explanations on many questions, and I very much appreciate the replies received from those who kindly responded. It is impossible to thank all of them individually, but I would like to single out the following for special mention as they provided me with important pieces of written or oral information:

David Alun Jones, D. Geraint Lewis & Dr Lionel Madden (Aberystwyth); Rob Culley (Ammanford Town FC); Cllr. Glynog Davies (Brynaman); Alison Carrington, Cllr. Mike Bartlett & David Jayne (Brynithel); Y Parchg Elwyn Pryse (Bow Street); Paul Davies & Carole Shone (Buckley Society); Carol Cole & Jeremy Griffiths (Carew FC); David Collins (Cardiff); Roy Bergiers, Cllr. Peter Hughes Griffiths & Peter Harding (Carmarthen); Peter Evans (Cogan Coronation FC); Paul Clement (Dafen Welfare FC); Meurig Morris (Evans & Williams Sports FC); Stan Strickland (CPD Glantraeth FC); John Damon (CPD Harlech Town FC); Martin Phillips (Killay FC); Dennis Jones (Llandysul); Alun Mummery, Steve Smith & William Williams (CPD Llanfairpwll FC); John Roberts (CPD Llangefni FC); Simon Botley (Llanymynech FC); Eifion Parry (CPD Nefyn FC); Gari Lewis & Ritchie Jenkins (CPD Penrhyn-coch FC); Dave Randall (AC Pontymister FC),

Karen Pearson (Rhyl Hearts FC); Anthony Jervis (Seaside FC); Tom Price (North Cornelly); Eirian Reynolds (Sêr Ceredigion DFC); Gwyn Jenkins (Tal-y-bont); Cllr. Cari Morgans (Tonna); Cllr. Rebeca Lewis (Trebanos); Alun Davies, Delyth & Geraint Morgan (CR Tregaron RFC); Steven Broome (Treharris Athletic Western FC); Ryan Romans (Wattstown RFC); Ray Jones (West End United FC); and Gareth Williams (West Wales FA).

In addition to these sources much useful information was gleaned from Wikipedia entries, Facebook pages, local history websites, club websites and the websites of the various leagues and associations in the Welsh football and rugby pyramids.

In particular, the website of the Welsh Football Data Archive (www.wfda.co.uk) and its indefatigable creator Mel Owen was especially useful in dating the existence of several teams who are no longer in existence. Current and archived copies of local newspapers, and their digital and on-line counterparts, also provided a rich source of match reports and press nicknames. The pages of that excellent periodical *Welsh Football*, and its regular features on local clubs was an inspirational source of many anecdotes which have been incorporated into this volume – the contributions of David Collins and Stuart Townsend were especially informative. Similarly, the magazine *Welsh Rugby* also proved a fruitful source of information. The *Dictionary of the place-names of Wales*, by Hywel Wyn Owen & Richard Morgan, also proved invaluable, and provided a standard guide to correct orthography.

I have also added two indexes which I hope will make the work more useful – the first, an index to all the clubs mentioned in the text, with a cross-reference to the relevant paragraph. The second index lists personal and corporate names recorded in the text, again with a reference to the relevant entry. A bibliography of printed material consulted has also been added to the appendices.

Finally, I wish to thank my wife Eirlys for her support and for reading a draft of this work and for making many helpful suggestions. Shaun Tyas has also read several drafts of the work, and made many useful suggestions for improvements. Any errors that remain are entirely my responsibilty.

Richard E. Huws,
rehuws@aol.com

THE DICTIONARY

Academicals / Accies: Cardiff Academicals FC. Known by the nickname *Accies*, the team play in the Cardiff & District League. The name is more famously associated with the Scottish team, **Hamilton Academical FC,** and predictably there is a connection. Apparently, Hamilton's score was being broadcast on television at the same time as a group of friends in Cardiff were discussing the possibility of forming a football team in 1979; the name appealed, and the group decided that *Academicals* would be adopted as a suffix for their new team. As the group included budding solicitors Simon Mumford and Paul Warren, this might be an additional reason why the suffix *Academicals* was chosen. Their first match, a friendly, was played against the students of the Law Society of University College, Cardiff, and the team played their first league match in September 1979. In Hamilton's case, the name *Academical* arose as they were established in 1874 from the school football team at Hamilton Academy. They remain the only mainstream professional club in British football to have originated as a school team. The **Welsh Academicals XV RFC,** also nicknamed the *Accies*, is a team formed in 1927, which is composed of Welsh students studying at universities and colleges throughout the United Kingdom, who have represented Wales in tournaments such as the Hong Kong 7s.

Aces: AC Pontymister FC. A nickname which derives from the AC, Athletic Club, element of the club's name. The enforced closure of the club's ground in 1997 by the local authority resulted in a move to their current home of Pontymister Recreation Ground which was donated for community use by Lord Tredegar, and not for any sole sporting organisation. This, apparently, accounts for the adoption of the prefix AC by the football team. The nickname *Aces* is widely used and also features on the club's matchday programmes. *See also:* **Roger Aces**

Adar Gleision *see:* **Bluebirds**

Adar Gleision Coch *see:* **Redbirds**

4

Aelwyd: Rhos Aelwyd FC. A suffix connected with the former Cymru Alliance team from Rhosllannerchrugog which was formed in 1943 at Jerusalem Welsh Presbyterian Church (Capel Mawr) where the *Aelwyd*, youth club of Urdd Gobaith Cymru, had met since its foundation by the Revd James Humphreys (1901–80) in 1941. The story relating to the founding of the youth club, which met some opposition from chapel elders, is told in the autobiography of Gwilym E. Humphreys (1932–80), a noted Welsh educationalist, and son of James Humphreys.

Airmen: Aber-porth FC. The nickname *Airmen* derives from the presence of the Royal Aircraft Establishment (RAE) in this Ceredigion coastal town. As a missile testing station, the team was also known as the *Rockets*.

Albies: Evans & Williams Sports FC. Founded in 1960 as **Evans & Williams United FC**, the team was originally drawn from the employees of the Llanelli-based wagon works, and it has enjoyed considerable success during its first 50 years of existence in the Carmarthenshire League. Enthusiastically encouraged by one of the firm's owners, Albert 'Albie' Evans (1902–68), the team soon acquired the nickname *Albies*. If the team lost, they were sometimes the butt of jokes along the lines that 'Evans turned up, but Williams didn't'. In 1967 the team's name was changed to **Evans & Williams Sports FC** to reflect its wider sporting interests which included cricket. The firm is no longer in business, but the family still retain their strong support for the club. Following his retirement as a professional footballer, the late Welsh international footballer Byron Stevenson (1956–2007) of Leeds United, Birmingham City and Bristol Rovers, played for two and a half seasons for the *Albies*.

Albion/s: A familiar suffix, being an archaic name for Britain, first used and popularised by **West Bromwich Albion FC**. **Scotch Albions FC** of Trealaw, one of the founder members of the South Wales League in 1890, was probably the first team to carry the name in Wales. Other Welsh teams that have carried the name include **Borras Park Albion FC, Cwm Albion FC** (who competed in the Southern League in 1911 but did not complete their fixtures), **Cwm Albion Colts FC, Garw Albions FC** (who operated in the 1920s), **Grange Albion FC, Splott**

Albion FC, Tonypandy Albion FC and **Ynys-hir Albions FC**.
Albion Rovers FC, based in Newport, and once of the Welsh League,
have an interesting history. They were formed in 1937 by migrant Scottish steel workers from Coatbridge, Lanarkshire. Because they endured
prejudice from existing local teams, they decided to form their own
club, taking the name of their local team **Albion Rovers FC,** formed
in 1882, and who still play in the Scottish Football League.

Alex (Alexandra): Mold Alexandra FC. The club was formed in
1929, evolving from a team run by a mission church. The suffix *Alexandra,* shortened to give the nickname *Alex,* was chosen, apparently,
because someone present at the inaugural meeting suggested the name
after picking up a hymn-book of the works of Cecil Frances Alexander
(1818–95), author of *All things bright and beautiful.* Her most famous
compilation, *Hymns for little children,* was first published in 1849. It
appears, therefore, if this story is to believed, that it was not copied from
Crewe Alexandra FC, formed much earlier in 1877. The origins of
that name are also uncertain. In all probability, the club took its name
from a public house, named the *Princess Alexandra* where early supporters of the club congregated, named after Princess Alexandra of Denmark
(1844–1925), who married the future King Edward VII (1841–1910).
Cardiff Alexandra RFC were founder members of the Cardiff &
District rugby union established in 1892; an earlier team **Alexandra
Rangers RFC,** of Newport, were formed in 1880–81.

All Blacks: A nickname most famously associated in Wales with **Neath
RFC**. The club's nickname, the *All Blacks (Crysau Duon)* or *Welsh All
Blacks,* comes from their iconic strip of black jerseys, shorts and socks
with a white Maltese cross. The origin of the team colours is uncertain.
Initially the club's players wore various dark kits and the cross pattée was
introduced by one of their players, thought to have been E. C. Moxham,
so as to break the monotony of the dark kits. It is believed that the strip
was later changed to an all black kit as a mark of respect for Richard
'Dick' Gordon, a player who died aged 27 years from injuries sustained
on the field of play against **Bridgend RFC** in 1880. This may account
for the *Mourners,* an early nickname given to the Club. The New Zealand
rugby team are famously known as the *All Blacks,* but it has been sug-

gested that the name was adopted much later than Neath after their European tour of 1905. **Tŷ-croes RFC** are also known as the *All Blacks* as are **Neyland RFC** who have also adopted a white fern as their emblem. **Cwm-carn United RFC** were also known as the *All Blacks* in the post 1945 period when they wore shirts which had been dyed black. The club website explains that the quality of the dye used was rather poor and had a habit of running in wet weather. This had the unfortunate effect of also dying the players black and as many were also colliers, the team became affectionately known as the *Cwm-carn All Blacks*. A team of motorbike enthusiasts, who played in an all-black kit, formed a team known as **Penparcau All Blacks FC** to compete in the North Cardiganshire Cup in 1966–67. They were the forerunners of **Barracudas FC**, who played briefly in the Aberystwyth & District Football League. *See also:* **Black/s; 'Ddu**

All Whites / Whites: A nickname which remains in common use and was prevalent in the early days of **Swansea RFC** as indicated by Argus' poem 'Hurrah for the *All Whites*', published in *The Cambrian* newspaper in 1886. However, the shirt colours first adopted by Swansea were blue with white horizontal stripes, before adopting a vivid scarlet shirt. The white jersey was later worn and retained, but the club did not truly become the *All Whites* until 10 January 1925 when white shorts were worn instead of the (usual) blue ones used previously. **Ammanford RFC, Kenfig Hill RFC** and **Llangennech RFC** were also known as the *All Whites* during their early days; however, they all later changed their colours. **Treharris FC**, founder members of the South Wales Association Football League were known as the *All Whites* or *Lilywhites*. More recently, probably due to the influence of the rugby culture in the Llyfni Valley, the suffix was adopted by **Caerau All Whites FC** who played in the Bridgend & District League, winning the Premier Division title on three occasions in the last twenty years. *See also:* **Lilywhites**

Alltudion *see:* **Exiles**

Alpha: Cardiff Corinthians FC. One of many nicknames enjoyed by this famous club, formed in 1898 when players from the Alpha Cricket Club decided to establish a football team to enable members to keep in touch during the winter months. *Alpha*, the first letter of the Greek alphabet, is used to indicate priority, and like *Corinthians*, pays homage to the Ancient World.

Amateurs: An early name adopted by **Caersws Amateurs FC** to enable the club to fire a shot across the bows of local rivals **Llanidloes Town FC** and **Newtown FC** who, unlike **Caersws FC** at the time, offered financial inducements to their players. The suffix Amateurs was dropped in 1974. **Taff's Well FC** were also known as the *Amateurs*. **Blaenau** (Ffestiniog) **Amateurs FC** were founded in 1980; however, the town has a very famous football tradition dating back to 1885, and has produced many famous players who have played at the highest level.

Amber & Blacks *see:* **Black & Ambers**

Ambers: *see:* **Black Ambers; Black & Ambers; Blue & Ambers; Claret & Ambers; Green & Ambers**

Am(m)an, Yr: Amman United RFC. A rugby team based in the industrial village of Glanaman, Carmarthenshire, which will always be associated with its most famous products: British Lions Shane Williams and Trevor Evans. Affectionately known as *Amman* or *Yr Aman*, the name is embodied in the club's song 'Yr Aman yw y gorau' [Amman is the best], and is derived from the name of the river Aman which flows through the village. The Club was the subject of a recent six-episode television documentary on S4C entitled *Clwb Rygbi Shane*.

Ancient Borough: Trebanos RFC. The derivation of the nickname is uncertain, but is thought to be connected with the local landed interests of Henry Somerset (*d.* 1646), 1st Marquess of Worcester.

Ancients, The: Cefn Druids FC. A nickname which probably acknowledges the early foundation of the club which dates back to the 1860s, and claims to be the oldest football club in Wales.

Antelopes: Llandegfan Antelope FC. The Anglesey League side are now known as the *Antelopes* following the merger of **Llandegfan FC** with **Antelope FC**, a former Sunday League team based at the *Antelope*

Inn, a public house located on the mainland side of the Menai Suspension Bridge in Gwynedd. The merger took place in July 2012, and the new team, who display an antelope on their club crest, play at Llandegfan, a village located between Menai Bridge and Beaumaris. **Antelope FC** play in the Merthyr Tudful League and are based at the *Antelope Inn*, Dowlais.

Arabs: Arabs FC were a successful Aberystwyth University students' team during the period 1966–73, reaching three League Cup finals during this era. The origin of the name is unknown.

Arcadians: Holywell Arcadians FC, were a successful team competing in the Welsh League in the 1930s. *Arcadia* was one of the administrative units of Ancient Greece, and the term has strange poetical mystical associations which might account for the name being chosen.

Archers: Cardiff Metropolitan FC / RFC. A nickname associated with both rugby and football codes played by teams representing Cardiff Metropolitan University (formerly UWIC and Cardiff College of Education). The nickname *Archers* is thought to derive from the significant rôle played by Welsh archers at the Battle of Crécy in 1346. An archer has always appeared on the clubs' emblems, and is still prominently displayed by **Cardiff Metropolitan RFC** on their website. The description 'crapping archer' has been used by generations of students when referring to the emblem. *See also:* **Black Army**

Arky: Penparcau FC. A nickname used on the club's own website in match reports, and on message boards by the club's opponents. It is derived from *Penarky,* a disparaging variation of *Penparke,* the anglicized form and pronunciation of this village, which is now an integral part of Aberystwyth.

Athletic: A common suffix for football teams which often reflects an initial association with athletics or youth clubs, which was the case with **Charlton Athletic FC** and Spanish giants **Athletic Club Bilbao** and **Atlético Madrid.** The most famous Welsh team to carry the name was **Aberdare Athletic FC**, who played in the Third Division of the Football League for six seasons until 1927. Some rugby teams also carry the suffix, notably **Bridgend Athletic RFC** and **Carmarthen Athletic RFC.**

Babes: Llandysul FC. A nickname prevalent for the club during the 1960s, possibly derived from the 'Busby Babes' of **Manchester United** FC, a description coined by the *Manchester Evening News* to describe the fine team of young home grown players, eight of whom perished in the Munich air disaster in 1958.

Bad Boys: Defaid Du FC. [Black Sheep FC]. The team, who entered the Montgomeryshire League in 2004, played at Llandrinio, Powys. Their imaginative Welsh name, sometimes translated as *Bad Boys*, was apparently based on the fact that many of their players had less than spotless criminal records!

Badgers: In the case of **Pont-y-clun RFC** the nickname reflects their playing colours of black and white hoops, and a badger also appears on the club's emblem. **Blaenau RFC**, who play on the outskirts of Ammanford, are also nicknamed the *Badgers,* although their main colours are green. The badger also features on their club badge. **Blaenau RFC**'s excellent website offers two explanations for the *Badgers* nickname. The first, and happier version, relates to a badger being knocked down by the team bus on the way back from Lampeter, and after being picked up by two of the players and nursed back to full health it was released back into the wild! The second, similar version, relates to another badger, again being knocked down by the team bus, but which did not survive. The bus-driver managed to produce a spade, and a fully-fledged funeral with Welsh hymns was held on a grass verge by the players somewhere between the West Country and West Wales!

Baglan Bombers: Baglan RFC. Formed in 1962, this Port Talbot-based rugby club has enjoyed a good deal of success including winning the Welsh Brewers' Cup in 1983 and 1984. It gained WRU status in 1995.

Banc: Bancffosfelen FC. An abbreviation of the Gwendraeth Valley village's name, and a team that has a fine football tradition.

Banw: Dyffryn Banw FC. An abbreviation of the place-name, reflecting the name of the river Banw.

'Banws : Trebanos RFC. The etymology of the place-name is uncertain. The mutated element *ban* could be the plural form *panos*, meaning cotton grass, while it has also been suggested that the name is derived from the elements *tre* (town) + *banos* (crows), associated with the large rookery situated above the Old Darren Colliery. In 1952, the club, which was founded in 1897, commissioned a new emblem, and following a competition, the design entered by Mr Tal Williams, a schoolmaster and rugby referee, incorporating two rooks, was deemed the winner, and subsequently adopted.

Barracudas: Barracudas FC were a short-lived Aberystwyth & District Football League team who played from 1967 to 1968, folding at the end of the 1971–72 season. They evoved from the **Penparcau All Blacks FC**, a team that was formed to compete in the North Cardiganshire Cup in 1966–67. The name Barracudas was chosen because of their enthusism for motorcycles – the *BSA C25 Barracuda* being a popular model at the time. The *barracuda* is a predatory tropical fish with vicious teeth, and the name also served to warn the opposition of what could be expected from them on the football field!

Barrians: Barry RFC's second XV play under this name.

Batchelors: The foundations of rugby football were laid at Penarth with the formation of the local rugby club, Penarth Football Club, during the 1879–80 season. The club was a privately formed venture by the Batchelor family, one of the town's affluent industrial families whose wealth derived from the booming coal trade in the town's docks. Founded by Cyril Batchelor, the **Batchelors' XV,** as they were familiary known, amalgamated with the **Penarth Dreadnoughts RFC** in 1885, eventually evolving into the modern **Penarth RFC.**

Batmans: Newtown FC. An unofficial nickname popularised by the Batman films, of the late 1980s and 1990s and a pun on the official nickname *Robins* (Batman being Robin's crime-fighting partner).

Bay Enders: Cemaes Bay FC. The club had a troubled existence, especially during its short tenure in the League of Wales from 1995 to 1998. It slipped in soap opera fashion from one crisis to another, earning itself the nickname **Bay Enders,** a pun on *Eastenders*, and a name coined by Cemaes fan Gareth Jones, a *Holyhead & Anglesey Mail* photo-journalist.

Bears: A name famously associated with American football giants **Chicago Bears.** There are some examples of its use in Wales: **Ammanford Bears FC**, were a non-denominational team founded by a Catholic priest in 1950 which competed for many seasons in the local football league. It is not inconceivable that the suffix *Bears* is an error for *boars* as the town has a close association with the legend of the *Twrch Trwyth*. **CPC Bears RLFC** are a regional amateur rugby league team, based in Carmarthen, representing Carmarthenshire, Ceredigion and Pembrokeshire.

Beaus, The: Beaumaris Town FC. The name is an abbreviation of Beaumaris. The town's name is derived from the Norman French *beau* + *maris* meaning 'fair marsh', on which the impressive Edwardian concentric castle was built in the latter years of the thirteenth century.

Beavers: Rhyl FC. A nickname prevalent in the 1980s derived from the name of the club's ground, Belle Vue.

Beeg: Aberbeeg RFC. A nickname based on an abbreviated version of the place-name. *Beeg* is derived from the Welsh *Big,* the river name which features in an anglicised form in the place-name.

Beganifs: Waunfawr FC. *Beganifs* is a derogatory nickname given to the residents of Waunfawr, Gwynedd, and is still used in the local press in relation to the local football team, **Waunfawr FC.** The nickname was popularised by three local boys from the village who formed the very successful Welsh pop group *Beganifs* in 1988 – they later changed the name to *Big Leaves*. The origins of the nickname are uncertain. R. Gwynn Davies has argued that *Beganifs* is derived from an unruly petty criminal named Wil Began (his mother was **Began If**an) who spent some time behind bars for his minor transgressions. Indeed, the whole family demonstrated the same traits and were soon baptized by all in the community as the *Beganifs* – a name which eventually spread to include all the residents of Waunfawr. Dilwyn Grey-Williams rejects this theory arguing that the name is derived from a woman named **Megan If**(an) Dafydd who was a leading Methodist and feminist. Grey-Williams believes that the name was coined by supporters of the Anglican Church in Caernarfon to denigrate their nonconformist neighbours in Waunfawr.

Berries: CPD Llanberis FC. An early local press nickname, where the mutated name of Saint Peris was anglicized to *Berries*.

Black Ambers: Builth Wells FC. The name reflects their playing colours of amber shirts and black shorts. **Crook Town FC**, of County Durham, the famous English non-league team, once shared this form of the nickname, but they are now known as the *Black & Ambers*.

Black & Ambers: The famous colours of **Newport RFC** may owe their origins to the influx of labour from the English Midlands to work in the local iron industry. These men came mainly from the Wolverhampton area, and their football team played in old gold and black. When **Newport County FC** was founded in 1912 they also adopted the same colours, and their supporters are known as the *Amber Army*. The nickname *Black & Ambers* is also shared by **Kidwelly RFC, Pontarddulais RFC** and **Skewen RFC**, three former centres of heavy industry, and by **Canton RFC. Aberaeron FC** are known as the *Black & Ambers* and **CPD Llanberis FC** are also known as *Y Blac & Amber*. **Berriew FC** have been referred to as the *Amber & Blacks*.

Black & Blues: Llanharan RFC. Traditional supporters prefer to use the nickname *Black & Blues*, rather than the more modern *Dairymen*. The choice of colours is said to relate to the club's impoverished early days when a sympathetic **Cardiff RFC** gave them a set of their kit, and the black and Cambridge Blue has been worn ever since by **Llanharan RFC**. In respectful appreciation Llanharan called themselves the *Black & Blues* as opposed to the *Blue & Blacks*, adopted by **Cardiff RFC.**

Black & Green: **Aberystwyth Town FC.** A traditional nickname reflecting the club's playing colours, and a description used in the title of their centenary volume *The Old Black & Green*, published in 1987. The book notes that '**Aberystwyth Town** adopted black & green harlequin at the start of the 1893–94 season when D. L. 'Dai Locke' Davies, manager of Messrs Downie's presented the club with a new set of shirts'.

Black & Tans: An early nickname for **Seven Sisters FC** who entered the Aberdare Football League in 1929, and were the forerunners of the present team who once played in the Welsh League. The team have long played in green shirts and **Seven Sisters FC** have now slipped down in the pyramid and play in the Neath Football League. The nickname arose from their original club colours, and is almost certainly derived from the notorious *Black & Tans* employed as an auxiliary force by the Royal Irish Police to suppress the Republican dissidents during the period 1920–21.

Black & Whites: Blaenavon RFC and **Chepstow RFC.** The nickname reflects the playing colours of both clubs.

Black Army: Llantrisant RFC. The origins of the nickname can be traced to the fourteenth century when the Lord of Glamorgan raised an army of archers from Llantrisant to fight for the King's son, Edward, the Black Prince (1330–76), at the Battle of Crécy in 1346. The Llantrisant men displayed great valour and courage, and were named the *Black Army* in recognition of their heroic exploits.

Black Cats: The nickname of **Kidwelly FC**, from the black cat which features on the arms of Kidwelly borough. There are several theories as to why this is so. The most popular is the belief that a black cat was the first creature seen alive after the Black Death hit the town in 1361, but by whom is not recorded! It was therefore honoured as a symbol of salvation and deliverance and subsequently used as Kidwelly's heraldic symbol. **Sunderland FC** also share this nickname, but the origins of the *Black Cats* of Wearside can be traced much later, to the time of the Napoleonic wars of the early nineteenth century when a black cat frequented a military look-out post, and frightened one of the personnel with its constant wailing.

Black Dragons: Nickname of **Banwen RFC** and **AFC Porth** [briefly **AFC Rhondda**]. The *dragon* is a symbol of Welsh identity, and the colour *black* signifies coal, as depicted on the heraldic arms of the Rhondda Borough Council. *See also:* **Dragons**

Black Sheep *see:* **Bad Boys**

Blackbirds: An early nickname associated with **Betws FC** (Ammanford). This is presumably based on the black and white striped shirts worn by the team, although there is no white on a blackbird. **Betws FC** was founded at the end the Second World War, but a team known as the **Betws Blackbirds FC** had played during the 1930s. **Betws FC** entered the Welsh League in 1949, changing its name to **Ammanford Town FC** in 1960. In 1992 the club amalgamated with **Ammanford Athletic FC** to become **Ammanford FC**, a club which still plays in the original Betws colours of black and white.

Blacks: Burry Port RFC. A nickname accorded to a team that play in an all black kit. **Seven Sisters RFC** were also once known as the *Blacks*, but they now play in green, white and black shirts with black shorts. *See also:* **All Blacks; Blue & Blacks; Green & Blacks; Green, White & Blacks; Red & Blacks**

Blast: Pontlottyn Blast Furnace FC. A Rhymney Valley club who played in the Welsh League from 1977 until 2003, and were known as the *Blast*, a name which reflects the village's importance as an early centre of the iron industry in Wales.

Blue & Ambers: Gilfach Goch RFC. This is a reflection of the club's playing colours and the name of its Vice Presidents' Club.

Blue & Blacks: Cardiff RFC. Founded in 1876, the club originally wore a black strip with a skull and crossed-bones on the front, which reflected Cardiff's 'murky past as a haunt of pirates and wreckers who preyed on the rich merchant venturer trade of the Bristol Channel'. However, when parents complained about the inappropriate emblem, a new strip was chosen within a year. A Cambridge college student from the area, Thomas Williams Rees, was familiar with the university colours of blue & black and the colours were subsequently adopted as Cardiff's new strip. Henceforth the club would be known as the *Blue & Blacks*. *See also:* **Black & Blues; Skull & Crossbones**

Blue & Whites: Pyle RFC. The nickname reflects the club's playing colours of blue and white hoops.

Blue Bulls: Bridgend Blue Bulls RLFC are a rugby league side based at the South Road ground of Porth-cawl RFC. They are considered to be the most successful amateur rugby league team in Wales. The name may owe its origins to the famous South African **Blue Bulls** rugby union team of the Northern Transvaal, better know by their Afrikaans name *Die Blou Bulle*. *See also:* **Bulls**

Blue Dragons: Cardiff City Blue Dragons RLFC. A second division rugby league team based at Ninian Park, Cardiff, which played for three seasons from 1981 with limited success. They were forced into liquidation in 1984, but were resurrected by a new consortium and renamed **Bridgend Blue Dragons RLFC**, after relocating to Coychurch Road, the former home of **Bridgend Town FC.** The club finished bottom of the league and folded after one season. *See also:* **Dragons**

Blue Stars: Port Talbot Blue Stars FC. *See also:* **Stars**

Bluebirds (Adar Gleision): A nickname most famously associated with **Cardiff City FC**. It is believed that the name was adopted after the club played its first game at Ninian Park on 1 September 1910 when they wore blue shirts. The nickname *Bluebirds* was adopted shortly afterwards and may be attributable to the enormous popularity of a play performed at Cardiff's New Theatre, entitled *The Blue Bird* by Maurice Maeterlinck (1862–1949), a Belgian playwright, who was awarded the Nobel Prize for Literature in 1911. Recently the club announced its highly controversial decision to play in red during 2012–13, using an amended emblem which relegates the traditional bluebird symbol and gives precedence instead to a Red Dragon. Other clubs known as the *Bluebirds* include **Abertillery Bluebirds FC, Brithdir Bluebirds FC, Caersws FC, Cardiff City Ladies LFC, Dafen Welfare FC, Haverfordwest County FC, Narberth FC** and **Trethomas Bluebirds FC.** Although **Dafen Welfare FC** was formed in 1925, two years before **Cardiff City FC** won the FA Cup in 1927, there is no foundation to the myth that the Dafen nickname dates from that period. It was popularised in the 1970s by Gary Martin, a schoolteacher and the club's centre half. Rugby club **Glais RFC,** also known as the *Bluebirds,* originally played in green and gold, before adopting blue and white hoops, and finally settling on blue shirts.

Blues (Gleision): The nickname adopted by many teams who play in blue shirts, or blue and white hoops. These include rugby sides **Bargoed RFC, Cardiff Blues RFC, Cwmllynfell RFC, Glais RFC, Haverfordwest RFC, Loughor RFC, Penarth RFC, Clwb Rygbi Rhuthun / Ruthin** and **Ystradgynlais RFC. Treorchy RFC,** founded in 1886, played in royal blue, and were known as the *Blues* until they adopted their present colours, black and white hoops, in 1889. Welsh football teams who share the *Blues* name, famously associated with **Birmingham City FC** and **Everton FC,** include **Amlwch Town FC, Bargod Rangers FC, Bettws FC, Blaenavon Blues FC, Goytre FC, Maesglas FC** of Cardigan, **Port Talbot FC, Ruthin Town FC** and **Seaside FC,** of Llanelli. **Oswestry Town FC,** formerly of the League of Wales, were also known as the *Blues* prior to their merger with **Llansantffraid FC.** *See also:* **Black & Blues; Boys in Blue; Sky Blues**

Boars: *see:* **'Twrch; Wild Boars.**

Bobbies: A nickname for football and rugby teams fielded by police forces. e.g. **Monmouthshire Police RFC.** The name is derived from Sir Robert Peel (1788–1850) who as Home Secretary created the modern police force. *See also:* **Boys in Blue**

Boded: CPD Bodedern Athletic FC. *Boded* is an abbreviation of the village name, more commonly used following a Christian name to designate a native of the village.

Bois y Llan: Llangennech RFC. This village club on the outskirts of Llanelli is known as *Bois y Llan,* as noted in the title of the club's centenary history by Kenny Bevan, published in 1987.

Bombers / Bombettes: Barry RFC are nicknamed the *Bombers.* The origin is uncertain, but may be connected with Michael Smyth (*b.* 1970), the Welsh welterweight boxing champion who was nicknamed the *Barry Bomber.* When **Barry Ladies** rugby team was formed in 2010 they became known as the *Bombettes. See also:* **Baglan Bombers**

Bont: A popular mutated abbreviation for a number of village teams which include the element *pont* (*bridge*). These include *Y Bont* for **Pontarddulais RFC** and *Bont* for **Pontrhydfendigaid & District FC.** *See also:* **Bridge; Pont**

Bony: Bôn-y-maen RFC. An abbreviated form of the place-name Bôn-y-maen.

Borderers / Borderettes: A nickname shared by **Whitland RFC** (their ladies' team is known as the **Borderettes**) on the Carmarthenshire / Pembrokeshire border, and **Knighton Town FC** on the Powys / Hereford & Worcester border, and notably **Berwick Rangers FC**, an English club, who play in the Scottish Football League.

Bordermen: The nickname of recently revived **Llanymynech FC** (also known as the *Exiles*), a split village on the Powys / Shropshire border, and **Saltney Town FC** on the Flintshire / Cheshire border, a new and successful club formed in 2010 who play in the Welsh National League. The nickname is shared with **Newry City FC** who straddle the Northern Ireland / Republic of Ireland border.

Boro: An abbreviation of *Borough,* as applied famously to **Middlesbrough FC.** It has been recorded for some Welsh teams, notably **Borough United FC** and **Pembroke Borough FC.**

Boys in Blue: The nickname of the **South Wales Police RFC**, reflecting their uniform colours, but one which is also shared with Irish rugby teams **Garryowen RFC** and **Leinster Rugby.**

Brake Liners: The name and nickname of the works team drawn from the Ferodo brake linings factory at Caernarfon which competed for three seasons in the Caernarfon & District Football League from 1964 until 1967.

Brân / Brain *see:* **Crows**

Bravehearts: Swansea City Bravehearts DFC. An aptly named special needs football team founded in 2000 and which now has around 100 members. *Braveheart* is the name given to the thirteenth-century Scottish hero William Wallace (*c.*1270–1305) in the 1995 film of the same name in which he is shown courageously fighting and dying for Scottish independence. *Bravehearts* has also been recorded as a nickname for the Scottish national football team.

Brewers: Rhymney RFC. A nickname associated with the famous Rhymney Breweries Ltd., once the largest brewery business in Wales which had operated for 140 years prior to its acquisition by Whitbread in the 1960s. The nickname is shared with Football League team **Burton Albion FC**, based in the Staffordshire town of Burton-upon-Trent which is also famous for its breweries.

Brewery Boys: A relatively new nickname for **Bridgend Town FC**, used by the press since their move to the Brewery Field, Bridgend, home of **Bridgend Ravens RFC**.

Bricklayers: The nickname of **Grange Stars RFC**, a Cardiff & District rugby team which operated in the period prior to the Great War. Based in the Cardiff suburb of Grangetown, known as the 'City of Bricks' owing to its large number of brick-built houses providing accommodation for its working-class population, the rugby team soon acquired the nickname *Bricklayers*.

Bridge: A nickname shared by **Bridgend Town FC** and **Newbridge RFC**. An abbreviation of the place-names, both clubs have also incorporated a bridge into their club emblems. **Merlin's Bridge FC** is also often referred to as the *Bridge*. *See also:* **Bont; Pont**

Bridgemen: Newbridge-on-Wye FC. The nickname of the successful Powys village club which also depicts a bridge on its club emblem.

Brocks: Hirwaun RFC. According to the Penderyn-born poet and printer Jenkin Howell (1836–1902), writing in 1900, the residents of Hirwaun were known as *brocks* – the name of a breed of black and white mountain pony that once inhabited the *gwaun* or moor. The name lives on as the nickname of the rugby club which has incorporated the pony as its emblem. The word *brock* is probably of English origin and is used to describe an inferior horse or trotter.

Broncos: Deri Broncos RFC and **Bon-y-maen Broncos RLFC,** a rugby league team formed in 2011, have both adopted this suffix popularised by the **Brisbane Broncos RLFC.** *Bronco,* a Spanish word, is a term used in northern Mexico, United States and Canada to denote an untrained horse.

Brotherhood: Hafod Brotherhood FC. The *Brotherhood* are the longest serving team in the Swansea Senior League. The Hafod Brotherhood was founded in 1910 by the Revd Thomas Langdon Rogers (1877–1966) and was originally part of the United Methodist Church in St. Thomas', Swansea, but later moved to its present building in Odo Street (now the Hafod Islamic Cultural Centre), where it once boasted an orchestra and lively non-denominational services. Rogers, born in Cambridgeshire, served at Swansea from 1909 to 1912. He died at Poole, Dorset in 1966. The football club was established in 1922, and although it still retains its original name, it has no connection with the small Christian group which still struggles to maintain the name of the *Brotherhood*, and now concentrates solely on fundraising, after its building was acquired as an Islamic Learning Centre. The Hafod Brotherhood Bowling Club established in 1927, is located at the northern end of Odo Street.

Bucks: Buckley Town FC. An abbreviation of Buckley – the club is also known by the nicknames *Claymen* and *Trotters*. The head of a buck, the male of an antlered animal such as the deer, appears on the club's crest. Scholars now tend to agree that Buckley derives from an Old English personal name *Bocca,* rather than from the Old English *bucc,* meaning deer, although there is evidence of a local deer park in the area created by Roger de Monhault, and destroyed by Llywelyn ap Gruffydd in 1257.

Buds: Aberbargoed Buds FC. *Buds* is believed to be an acronym for *Bedwellty Urban District Sides.*

Bulldogs: A name most famously associated in Wales with **Ton Pentre FC**, sometimes also known as the *Rhondda Bulldogs.* The club's crest also incorporates a *bulldog.* **Vista FC**, a community club who play in the Cardiff Combination League, were formerly known as **Llanedeyrn Bulldogs FC** until the name changed in 2011. **Blackwood Bulldogs RLFC** were formed in 2006. *See also:* **Scarlet Bulldogs**

Bulls: Several teams in Wales carry this name, which is also the well-known nickname of **Bradford Bulls RLFC. Builth Wells RFC**, founded in 1888, is nicknamed the *Bulls*, reflecting the agricultural origins of the town. The place-name *Builth* is a corruption of the Welsh *buallt*, meaning 'cow pasture', and the club's crest shows a bull, charging through rugby posts. It is believed that the original Builth bull was white; however, a life-size sculpture of a Welsh Black bull by local sculptor Gavin Fifield was unveiled at Builth in November 2005 to underline the animal's historic connection with the town. It stands as an impressive feature in the Groe, a riverside park, close to the rugby ground. **Builth Wells FC** are also known as the *Bulls*, and the animal also features on the club's crest. Anglesey Football league clubs of the 1960s **Bryngwran Bulls FC** and **Llannerch-y-medd Bulls FC** are other examples of the name, and both suffixes were derived from the public houses where the teams had their headquarters. **Clwb Rygbi Nant Conwy** is also nicknamed the *Bulls.* **Swansea Bulls RLFC**, formed in 2002, developed into **Swansea Miners RLFC**. *See also:* **'Bŵl, Teirw Duon, Teirw Nant Conwy**

'Buns: A nickname shared by **St. Alban's RFC,** Tremorfa, Cardiff, and **Ynys-hir Albions,** being compressions of *Alban's* and *Albions.*

Burglars: Kenfig Hill Juniors FC were a senior team which played in the Port Talbot & District League from 1936 to 1939. Allan Brookes notes that 'the team were sometimes naughtily nicknamed the *Burglars* by their opponents, owing to the spate of burglaries occurring in the buildings surrounding their playing field, which were often in a terrible state of repair'.

Butcher Boys *see:* **Donkey Island Butcher Boys**

Butchers: Abergavenny Thursdays FC. This Monmouthshire club with an illustrious history is known by several nicknames. *Butchers* is a nickname which can be attributed to the significance of the town's famous cattle market.

Butchers' Arms Boys: Pontypridd RFC. The nickname relates to the public house in Taff Street, Pontypridd where James Edward Spickett (1859–1919), a young lawyer, who later captained the club, together with Walter Morgan, chief clerk to the county court house, organised a meeting in 1877 to form a rugby team in the town. Local historians Gareth Harries and Alan Evans used the title *The Butchers' Arms Boys* in their club centenary publication issued in 1977.

'Bŵl: A similar compression to that found in *'Buns*, above, has give us the nickname *'Bŵl* for **Ynys-y-bŵl RFC.** *The Dictionary of place-names of Wales* notes that *Bŵl* is derived from the Middle English *boule* (bowl), and may refer in this context to the shape of the valley. **Ynys-y-bŵl FC** were also known as *'Bŵl* prior to their merger with **Pontypridd Town FC** in 1992. Both Ynys-y-bŵl clubs featured a bull on their club emblems, which shows that the nickname has further mutated to allow it to be represented visually as a bull, a pun on the sound of the place-name, but not its meaning.

Cam: Camrose FC. An abbreviation of the place-name, which is also recorded for **Cambrian & Clydach FC.**

Campers: Prestatyn FC. Recorded on *Seasiders' Online* in 2009, and suggested by a contributor as a much better nickname than the traditional and predictable *Seasiders*. It pays homage to the town's importance as a holiday and camping resort, and might also be appropriate on occasions when the team chose to camp in their own half in defensive mode.

Canaries: A nickname associated with several Welsh teams. **Caernarfon Town FC**, founded in 1876 as **Caernarfon Athletic FC**, became known as the *Canaries* due to their yellow shirts and green shorts, as reflected in the title *The Canaries sing again*, chosen for the club's history written by Ian Garland and Wyn Gray-Thomas and published in 1986. The bird also appears on the club's crest. However, the origin of the nickname *Canaries* is unclear, but it had certainly been used for a long time as a name for the residents of Caernarfon, and is most likely a play on the letters contained in the place-name. This is confirmed in a report on a match played between **Llandudno Swifts FC** and **Carnarvon Ironopolis FC** and reported in the *North Wales Chronicle*, 26 January 1895. For a differing reason **Norwich City FC**, founded in 1902, has, since 1907, also been known as the *Canaries,* and the name and colours were originally chosen because of the proliferation of the practice of breeding the yellow cage bird in Norfolk. Other teams to carry the nickname include **Dolgellau FC, Montgomery Town FC** and the short-lived **Trefeurig & District United FC** who played for five post-war years in the Aberystwyth & District League in amber shirts, and were affectionately known as *Y Caneris Melyn*, or Yellow *Canaries*. **Alltwen RFC** were known as the *Canaries* during the 1920s and 1930s, before changing the colour of their kit.

Cape: Cymmer RFC. The upper reaches of the Afan Valley were once compared to the Cape of Good Hope in South Africa and the name has since been associated with the communities of Cymmer and neighbouring Blaengwynfi.

Cardis: Cardigan RFC. A *Cardi* is a nickname given to a person from Ceredigion (Cardiganshire).

Cards: Cardiff Corinthians FC. One of many nicknames enjoyed by this famous club, formed in 1898. *Cards* is an abbreviated form of Cardiff.

Carpets: A derogatory nickname applied to student rugby teams by their town neighbours, as they were there 'to be trodden on' by their opponents!

Castle: Caerphilly Castle LFC. Founded in 1999, the club is one of the leading female football teams in Wales, running a total of five teams for various age groups. The senior team competes in the Welsh National Premier League. The club takes its name from the town's Norman fortress, and its logo incorporates the castle's famous leaning tower.

Castlemen: A nickname applied to football and rugby teams who play in towns with well-known Norman fortifications. Examples recorded include **Beaumaris Town FC, Caerphilly RFC, Conwy Borough FC, Denbigh Town FC, Flint Town United FC, CPD Harlech Town FC** and **Rhuddlan Town FC**.

Castletown Men: An early nickname for **Caerphilly RFC**, based again on the importance of the town's magnificent fortification.

Cavaliers / Cavs: Nelson Cavaliers FC. The *Cavs* as they are sometimes known have an interesting motto, based on one of the quotations of Benjamin Franklin (1705–90): 'Fail to prepare – prepare to fail'. **Cavalier** was the name used by Parliamentarians for a Royalist supporter during the English Civil War. King Charles I visited the Nelson area in 1645 to seek the support of the local gentry families and called at the manor house of Llancaiach Fawr, but without much success. The village of Nelson derives its name from a public house reputedly called the *Lord Nelson* following his visit to the area in 1803. **Kenfig Hill RFC**'s second XV are also known as the *Cavaliers*.

Cefni: Llangefni FC / CR Llangefni RFC. Derived from the place-name *llan* (church) on the river Cefni.

Celtic / Celts (Celtiaid): A popular suffix, sometimes with Irish connotations, and influenced by the success of Glasgow's **Celtic FC**. Welsh teams that carry, or have carried, the suffix include **Abergele Celts FC, Cardiff Celts FC, Cwmbran Celtic FC** (originally formed in 1926 as the team of the Catholic Young Men's Society), **Llannerch Celts FC, Llechid Celts FC** and **Tal-y-sarn Celts FC,** who are also referred to as *Celtiaid*. In rugby circles **Maesteg Celtic RFC** have adopted the suffix.

Cennech: Llangennech RFC. Abbreviation of the place-name derived from St. Cennych or Cennech.

Chancers: A suffix used by the second XV of Bettws RFC.

Cheesemen: Caerphilly RFC. The nickname is a reference to the famous white cheese, that originated in the area around the town of Caerphilly where it was first sold by farmers in the local market. It is thought that the cheese was first developed to provide local coal miners with a convenient way of replenishing the salt in their bodies lost after lengthy underground shifts. In England, **Cheddar FC** are also known as the *Cheesemen*.

Cherries: The nickname of Gwauncaergurwen based **Cwm-gors RFC,** founded in 1927, who play in cherry-coloured shirts and white shorts. **Furnace United RFC**, a club founded in 1883, and based on the outskirts of Llanelli are also known as the *Cherries*, and play in cherry & white hooped shirts. The nickname *Cherries* in rugby circles is famously associated with the mighty **Gloucester RFC**.

Cherry & Whites: A nickname shared by **Gorseinon RFC, Hendy RFC** and **Pontardawe RFC**, reflecting their club colours.

Chocolates: Llanfairpwll FC. The team was once known as *Y Chocolates* when they played for a brief period in brown shirts after the Great War. They later adopted black & white striped shirts, but currently play in blue & black shirts. The club, founded in 1899 as **Llanfair United FC**, has the longest name in world football – the full name of the village running to 58 letters. The club attracted a lot of attention on Brazilian television in 2012 because of its lengthy name.

CIACS: An acronym for Cardiff Internationals Athletic Club RFC, pronounced "Kayaks", a rugby team formed in 1946 in the Tiger Bay area of Cardiff docklands. The multicultural nature of the team is reflected in the name Internationals. The club is best known for having produced Billy Boston (*b*. 1934) who went on to become a rugby league legend and Great Britain international player in the 1950s.

Cil: Cilfynydd RFC. An abbreviation of the place-name meaning *nook* (cil) in the mountain.

Citizens (Y Dinasyddion): Bangor City FC. Developed from *city* and attributable to the cathedral city status of Bangor. *Dinasyddion*, the Welsh equivalent, is commonly used. The nickname *Citizens* is shared with **Manchester City FC**.

City of the Hills Boys: Bryn-mawr RFC. An early nickname for the Blaenau Gwent Club. Bryn-mawr, at 1250 to 1500 feet above sea level, is the highest town in Wales.

City Slickers: A nickname coined by Frank Wood, **Bangor City FC**'s programme editor, during the late 1960s and early 1970s when the team competed in the Northern Premier League. The nickname was also applied to **London Welsh RFC** during one of their more successful periods in the early 1970s, when they boasted several Welsh international players.

Civil: Newport Civil Service FC. A shortened form of the name.

Claret & Ambers: Abergavenny RFC. The team is so named due to their hooped claret and amber shirts. The club is also referred to as the *Clarets*.

Clarets: A nickname that reflects the colours of several famous clubs notably **Burnley FC. Churchstoke FC**, members of the Montgomeryshire League, are known as the *Clarets*. Other football clubs, such as **Killay FC** have opted to play in claret and blue because their founder, Bruce Roberts, was an avid fan of **West Ham United FC**!

Classics: Wrexham FC. A nickname applied to **Wrexham FC** by supporters of Rhosllannerchrugog as noted in a poem by *Rhosite* published in the *Rhos Herald*, 20 May 1922.

Claymen: Buckley Town FC. The name reflects the industrial history of the town, famous for the mining of both coal and heavy clay. The town boasted no fewer than fourteen kilns in the nineteenth century and became synonymous with the production of quality pottery and bricks.

Clowns: Pont-y-clun RFC. An early nickname for the club derived from a nineteenth-century form of the place-name, Pont-y-clown, named after a bridge over the river Clun, or Clown.

Coasters: Rhyl Coasters RLFC, formerly **North Wales Coasters RLFC** formed in 1989, an amateur rugby league club absorbed by the **Rhyl Exiles RLFC.**

COBRAS. Strictly an acronym which has developed into a nickname for **Caereinion Old Boys Rugby Association**, a club founded in 1978 by former pupils of Caereinion High School, Llanfair Caereinion, Powys. The club's emblem shows a cobra embroiled in a rugby post.

Cochion *see:* **Reds**

Cockerels: Two Welsh rugby teams are known as the *Cockerels*. **Heol-y-Cyw RFC**, founded in 1905, has a club badge which includes the image of a stone bridge and three chickens or *cockerels*. The emblem reflects the town's name which translates as 'the chick's road', derived from a lane that runs through the settlement. **Croesyceiliog RFC** are also known as the *Cockerels* – the village name translates as 'the cock's cross' and takes its name from an inn variously called *The Cock* and *Croes y Ceiliog*.

Cocklemen / Cockle Boys / Cockletown / Cocos: A nickname associated with teams from cockle picking areas such as **Pen-clawdd RFC**. It is inevitable that this village's rugby team, located on the Loughor estuary and world famous for its cockles, should have acquired a nickname associated with this industry, although it should be noted that the industry was predominantly operated by women rather than by men. **Pen-clawdd RFC** are now generally referred to as the *Cocklemen* (formerly *Cockle Boys*), but other less kind nicknames have also been associated with the team. Pen-clawdd residents were once called *Donks*, or *Donkeys*, by their posher neighbours on the Gower peninsula, a nickname borne from the use of the animal in gathering the valuable seafood. **Pen-clawdd FC** have two cockle shells on their club's emblem, but surprisingly, the cockle is not represented on the rugby club's motif. **Laugharne RFC**, another community with a strong cockling tradition and one of the oldest clubs in Wales, are also known as the *Cocklemen*, and were bitter rivals of Pen-clawdd. The **Laugharne RFC** team badge consists of a shield divided into quarters illustrating a cockle shell, a castle, a Celtic cross and a coat of arms which tell of Laugharne's links with the sea, its castle and its feudal and township system. The Portreeve of Laugharne also wears a chain of cockle shells. **Llangwm RFC**, Pembrokeshire, are another team who play in a village associated with the cockle industry. In all three instances the vociferous support once given by the cocklewomen to their battling rugby menfolk was notable and extremely intimidating to the opposition.

Beaumaris, Anglesey and Penrhyndeudraeth, Gwynedd, a town on the Dwyryd estuary are both known as **Cockletown**. More prevalent as a nickname for the town itself, *Cocklemen* has nevertheless been used to describe **Beaumaris Town FC** in the local press. However, in the predominantly Welsh-speaking town of Penrhyn-deudraeth, the form *Penrhyn Cocos* [Penrhyn Cockles] is a more familiar nickname for the residents, and was recorded in print as early as March 1890 in a nineteenth-century Welsh periodiocal, *Cyfaill yr Aelwyd*. The nickname *Cocos* has been applied to the local football team, **CPD Penrhyndeudraeth FC** and recorded in local community newspapers.

Cockney Welsh: A rather derogatory nickname applied to **London Welsh RFC**.

Cocos *see:* **Cocklemen**

'Coed: AFC Llwydcoed. An abbreviation of the place-name and used in local newspaper press reports featuring the Aberdare Valley team.

Cofis. Clwb Rygbi Caernarfon. The club is known as the *Cofis*, a word indicating natives of Caernarfon. *Geiriadur Prifysgol Cymru* notes that it is probably a borrowing from the English word *cove*, meaning a *chap or fellow*. The nickname *Cofis* is also applied to football teams from Caernarfon.

Collegians: A nickname once applied to student teams.

Colliers: A nickname acquired by several team who drew their players from coal mining villages. These include **Chirk AAA FC**, one of the earliest clubs in Wales, with players initially drawn from the local coal mining pits at Black Park and Brynkinallt collieries. Also known as the *Colliers* were **Gorsddu Rangers FC**, a club which played local football in the 1930s and drew its players from the Emlyn Colliery, Pen-y-groes, Carmarthenshire, a mine that operated from 1893 until its closure in 1939.

Colts: A popular suffix used by many youth teams and especially prevalent in the Swansea Senior League, as evidenced by the following examples: **Birchgrove Colts FC, Bon-y-maen Colts FC, Cwm Albion Colts, Kingsbridge Colts FC, Landore Colts Rangers FC, Plough Colts FC** and **Port Tennant Colts FC**. Although these teams compete in a senior league they also field a host of youth sides which provide useful academies for the senior sides.

Comets: Blackwood Stars RFC's second XV are known as the *Comets*.

Commandos *see:* **Valley Commandos**

Comrades: A popular suffix for football teams formed by soldiers who had survived the Great War. Examples include **Bangor Comrades FC, Bethesda Comrades FC, Blaenau Ffestiniog Comrades FC, Borth Comrades FC, Groeslon Comrades FC, Llanberis Comrades FC** and **Trevor Comrades FC**. Some of these teams may have been attached to social clubs affiliated to the Comrades of the Great War Association.

Cormorants: Tywyn / Bryn-crug FC. Tywyn FC merged with their neighbours **Bryn-crug FC** in 1989 to form **Tywyn / Bryn-crug FC**. The merged club, known as the **Cormorants,** includes the sea bird on its club's crest. The nickname is derived from the renowned inland breeding place for the Great Cormorant at neighbouring Craig yr Aderyn (Bird's Rock), a spectacular 800-foot-high rock outcrop in the Dysynni Valley. Cormorants are a common sight seen flying over the football field at Bryn-Crug.

Coronation: Cogan Coronation FC. Formed in 1961 and based at the Cogan Coronation Club, near Penarth from which the club derives its name, and where it is still based. The club was formed in 1937 by ship pontoon workers from Penarth Dock, and named in honour of the coronation of King George VI (1895–1952) in that year. The club crest was designed by Peter Evans in 1983, and incorporates several elements. The two birds featured are ravens, linked with Cogan from their association with the family crest of the Herbert family who were the principal local land owners. The crown represents the club's name, the dragon represents Wales, and the ship has been incorporated to signify the importance of Penarth Dock which was a major coal exporting port in the late nineteenth and early twentieth centuries.

Corries: An abbreviation of **Corinthians,** and probably adopted as a result of the early successes of **Corinthian FC**, the London based amateur club founded in 1882, who took their name from the Greek port of Corinth. Traditional Corinthian values were concerned with amateur participation and not fixated on winning or aspiring to professional status. **Brecon Corinthians FC**, **Cardiff Corinthians FC** and **Glyncoed Corries FC** are all Welsh teams known by this nickname. **Aberaman Corinthians** FC were also one of the first teams founded in South Wales.

Corrwg: Glyncorrwg RFC. An abbreviation of the place-name reflecting the name of the river Corrwg.

Cougars: The American mountain lion has been adopted as a suffix by **Cosheston Cougars FC,** a team formed in 2010 who compete in the

Pembrokeshire Football League, and who won promotion at the end of their first season, and prior to that by **Valley Cougars RLFC** (formerly **Cynon Valley Cougars RLFC**), a rugby league club now based at Caerphilly.

Cowboys: Inexplicably, the name has been recorded as a suffix for **Tir-y-dail Cowboys FC**, an Ammanford based team that played after the Great War, and for **Ebbw Vale FC**, first recorded in 1966.

Croesgadwyr *see:* **Crusaders**

Croesy: Croesyceiliog FC / RFC. An abbreviation of the place-name.

Crosses: Four Crosses FC. An abbreviation of the place-name.

Crows (Brân / Brain): The nickname *Crows* is associated with both **Cwmbrân Town FC** and **Cwmbrân RFC.** The name is derived from the place-name Cwm-brân which literally translates as 'valley of (the river) Brân'. *The Dictionary of the place-names of Wales* notes that the meaning of *brân* is 'crow or raven', and in this context possibly refers to dark waters rather than to a brook frequented by crows. The work also adds that Brân could be a personal name in this place-name. **Borth United FC**, formed in 1934, who play in the Aberystwyth & District Football League, are also known as the *Crows*, as reflected by the club's crest which shows a crow standing on a football. *Brain y Borth* [The Borth Crows] were considered the main local rivals to *Piod Bow Street* [Magpies of Bow Street FC]. **Rhos-goch Rangers FC**, of the Mid-Wales Football League are also known as the *Crows*, the nickname being derived from their ground located at Crow Lane, Rhos-goch, Powys.

Crusaders (Croesgadwyr): The name is based on the religious expeditionary wars of the eleventh to thirteenth centuries. **Crusaders RLFC** were a professional rugby league club based initially at Bridgend before moving to Wrexham. Originally known as the **Celtic Crusaders RLFC**, they succeeded after three seasons to obtain a licence to play in the Super League from 2009 to 2011. In July 2011 the club withdrew from Super League to compete in the next tier of the Rugby League Championship, changing its name to **North Wales Crusaders RLFC. Ynys-ddu Crusaders FC** play in the Gwent Football League.

Crwydriaid *see:* **Wanderers**

Crysau Cochion: Literally red shirts, and used for teams who play in those colours, and most notably the Welsh national rugby and football teams.

Crysau Duon *see:* **All Blacks**

Cuckoos: Risca United FC; Risca RFC. The nickname is derived from the ancient legend of the Risca cuckoo. The tale relates to the local inhabitants building a high hedge to prevent the cuckoo migrating back to Africa as it was thought that if it was retained the good weather would continue throughout the year. The tale has retained its appeal in recent children's books such as *Rhys and the cuckoo of Risca*, by Siân Lewis, issued in 1997. The cuckoo is represented on the badges of both Risca clubs. Roy D. Hacksaw, in his blog at http://boysinblackandwhite.blogspot.co.uk, has suggested that *Cuckoos* is an apt nickname for the football club as it has the knack of absorbing other teams whilst keeping its own identity intact.

Cynon: Abercynon RFC. An abbreviation of the name taken from the river Cynon.

Daffs / Daffodils / Super Daffs: Llanidloes Town FC. The well-known nickname of **Llanidloes Town FC**, a club with a rich history, is attributable to their playing colours of yellow shirts and green shorts. The daffodil, a symbol of Welsh national identity, is given prominence on the club's emblem which also records 1875 as the year when the club was founded. **Llanidloes RFC** also include the daffodil and the town's famous half-timbered market hall on their club emblem.

Dairymen: Llanharan RFC. The club play on Maes Llaethdy / Dairy Field, so named because of its proximity to the CWS milk depot which closed in the 1960s after half a century of processing. Consequently the team is nicknamed the *Dairymen*. The club's more traditional name is the *Black & Blues*.

Dale: Ferndale RFC. An abbreviation of the place-name. The club also has a fern on its emblem. The place-name Ferndale is a direct translation of Glynrhedynog, which translates as valley of the ferns. Ferndale was a name given to one of the pits sunk in the area in 1875.

Darans, Y: CPD Llanberis FC. A nickname with Biblical origins, from the Gospel according to St. Mark, Chapter 3, 17 relating to the appointment of the twelve disciples. 'And James the son of Zebedee, and John the brother of James; and he surnamed them Boangeres, which is, the sons of Thunder' *[Meibion y Daran]*. At a game between Felinheli and Llanberis held at Vaynol Park in the 1920s a humorous quarryman, with a good Biblical knowledge, shouted ' Come on the *Darans*' after witnessing the thunderous play of his football team, giving rise to the nickname which has featured in the title of Arwel Jones' club history, *Y Darans*, published in 1991. After this incident, witnessed by Huntley Edwards, a Llanberis supporter, the nickname was popularised and displaced the antiquated *Berries* in the local press.

Darians: Aberdare Town FC. The nickname is derived from the river *Dâr*, which meets the river *Cynon* at Aberdâr / Aberdare. **Aberdare Town FC** operated from 1934 until the outbreak of the Second World War. *Y Darian* [The Shield] was also the title of a radical newspaper published in Aberdare which championed the cause of the coal miners. It was first issued in 1875 as *Tarian y Gweithiwr* [The Workers' Shield], and its title was abbreviated to *Y Darian* in 1914. It ceased publication in 1934. **Aberaman FC** have since 2012 re-branded themselves as **Aberdare Town FC,** reviving the famous name from the past.

Dazzlers: The *Oxford English Dictionary* defines *dazzler* as 'a person or thing that dazzles, in particular a person who is overwhelmingly impressive or skilful', which makes it an appropriate nickname for a football team. It was used by a group of Carmarthen boys who formed a team in 1951, called **Dazzlers AFC**, to play friendly matches in the town and surrounding villages. They also produced a duplicated fanzine entitled

The Football Fan. *Dazzlers* was much later briefly adopted as the nickname of **Llangefni Town FC**. The name was coined by a group of local boys, including several university students, who formed a team to participate in an annual Easter Monday competition. *Dazzlers* may possibly have been chosen as the team name because the members dazzled academically! The competition attracted many teams with fascinating names, some of which are worth recording, such as **Crayston's Babes**, named in honour of the 1956–58 Arsenal manager Jack Crayston (1910–92).

'Ddu: Ynys-ddu RFC. The place-name translates as 'black water meadow' from the elements *ynys* + *du*. The club, which dates from 1884, originally played in an all black strip until the 1920s when they switched to red and black hooped shirts. However, they have retained the nickname *'Ddu*. See also: **Black/s**

Deesiders: Connah's Quay Nomads FC. The town lies on the river Dee in north-east Wales, and the team plays at the Deeside Stadium.

Defiants: Defiants FC. A team from the University College of Wales, Aberystwyth that competed in the Aberystwyth & District League for seven seasons from 1972 until 1979. The boldly resistant named team proved relatively successful and generally finished in mid-table.

Demolition Squad: Cemaes Bay FC. The nickname was adopted owing to an intimidating sign at the club's ground which stated 'Welcome to School Lane – home of the *Demolition Squad*'. Cheshire based Joe Davis, who headed a demolition firm was the club's chairman and main benefactor until his resignation in November 1997. King's Scaffolding Company of Liverpool also sponsored the club's shirts during 1995–96 when they played in the League of Wales.

Demons: Cardiff Demons RLFC. The *Demons* are an amateur rugby league club founded in 1997, and based in the Splott district of the city. It is a strange choice of suffix which is difficult to explain, but other examples in rugby circles exist, such as **Durham Demons RLFC** and **Northampton Demons RLFC**.

Dervishes: A nickname applied during the early years of **Canton RFC,** founded in 1877, and one of only four surviving teams from the original members of the Cardiff & District Rugby Union formed in 1892. The derivation of the nickname is unknown, but a *dervish* is defined as a sort of Muslim monk who might perform whirling dances and vigorous chanting as acts of ecstatic devotion.

Derwyddon *see:* **Druids**

Devils: The nickname of **Treherbert RFC** which is attributable to their playing colours of red shirts and black shorts. A Red Devil also appears on the club's emblem. **Aber-carn Devils RFC** are the club's second XV. **Dyffryn Devils RLFC,** based at Pen-y-banc, Carmarthen-shire, are an amateur rugby league team. *See also:* **Red Devils**

Dinasyddion *see:* **Citizens**

Dingle Boys: Tonna RFC. The nickname relates to one of the fields used by the club, which is now the Riverside Golf Range, Aberdulais. The land was once known as 'The Dingle'.

Div's: UWIC Inter Cardiff FC. Derived from the element *diff* in Cardiff.

Dockers: Swansea Dockers FC was originally formed in 1947 as **Swansea NDLB (National Docks Labour Board) FC**. The Board also provided financial support for the team which was drawn from the local dock work force. The name **Swansea Dockers** was adopted in 1950. **Dockers FC,** formed in 1986 by a group of **Cardiff City FC** fans, and reformed in 2004, is based at the Barry Dockers' Sports & Social Club. The form *Dockites* has been recorded as a nickname for **Pembroke Dock Harlequins RFC** during the late nineteenth century.

Donkey Island Butcher Boys: Penarth RFC. An early club nick-name which is still occasionally heard. Initially games were played on land owned by David Cornwell (1841–1906), a Glebe Street master butcher, club benefactor and native of Cambridgeshire, on a field in Victoria Square where All Saints Church now stands. (The club's colours of blue and white, and its early nickname of *Blues*, derives from the butchers' apron). *Donkey Island* was a nickname given to the town of Penarth owing to the high number of locals who held a licence to operate donkey rides on the beach. However, the origins of *Donkey Island* may well date from the period prior to 1865 when the settlement was isolated and donkeys had to be used to bring goods and water to the residents from Cardiff via Leckwith Hill. Surrounded by water on three sides – the river Ely, the sea inlet at Cogan Pill, and the Bristol Channel, Penarth is to all intents and purposes an island.

Donkeys / Donks: Pen-clawdd RFC. Although they are now generally referred to as the *Cocklemen*, other names have also been associated with the team. Pen-clawdd residents were once known by the rather derogatory *Donks,* or *Donkeys*, by their posher neighbours, a name associated with the use of the animal in gathering the valuable seafood.

Draconians / Dracs: Cardiff Draconians FC. Derived from Draco, an Athenian law scribe who lived in the seventh century BC and who prescribed heavy punishments for relatively trivial offences. Another example of classicism, it is a strange choice of suffix, but it may have been chosen because it chimes with *Dragons.*

Dragons (Dreigiau): A popular nickname, based on a central creature in Welsh mythology, which has been adopted by a host of football and rugby teams, including the Welsh national football and rugby teams. Local football teams known as the *Dragons* include: **Abergele Dragons FC, Baglan Dragons FC, Barry Town FC, Mostyn Dragons FC, Pontypridd Town FC, West Dragons FC** and **Wrexham FC**, and now that **Cardiff City** have re-branded they may also be known as the *Red Dragons.* **Cardiff Dragons FC (CPD Ddreigiau** (*sic*) **Caerdydd)**, was formed in 2008 to promote participation in, and awareness of, football within the Gay community in Cardiff and beyond. **Afan Lido Dragons DFC** and **Merthyr Valley Dragons DFC** are pan disability football teams. **Mochdre Dragons DFC** is the only football club for deaf and hard of hearing players in north Wales, and only the second in Wales, the other being **Cardiff City Deaf DFC**. Rugby teams who have adopted the name *Dragons* include the regional side **Newport Gwent Dragons RFC [Dreigiau Casnewydd Gwent]** and **North Wales Dragons DRFC,** a wheelchair rugby side based at the Plas Madoc Leisure Centre, Wrexham. Other teams known as the *Dragons* include **Dowlais RFC** and **London Welsh RFC. South Wales Dragons RLFC** were established in 1995 and disbanded a year later. **Swansea / Llanelli Dragons RLFC** competed in 2010 in the South Wales Rugby League Championship. **Dee Valley Dragons RFLC** are an amateur rugby league team based at Corwen. *See also:* **Black Dragons; Blue Dragons; Red Dragons & Young Dragons**

Dreadnoughts: Penarth Dreadnoughts RFC. An early rugby team that amalgamated with the **Penarth [Rugby] Football Club** in 1885.

Dreigiau *see:* **Dragons**

Dreigiau Cochion *see:* **Red Dragons**

Drovers / Drover Boys (Y Porthmyn): Llandovery RFC. The nickname reflects the importance of Llandovery as an overnight stopping place for the cattle drovers on their tiring long journey to the market towns of the English Midlands. It has even been suggested that the first rugby ball was brought back to the town by the drovers from their travels to Blackheath where an early rugby club was founded in 1858. However, it is more likely that the game was first introduced into the town at Llandovery College, a public school founded in 1847. Nevertheless, the droving tradition accounts for the well-established nickname of the rugby club. A wealthy drover, David Jones (*d.* 1739), established the first private bank in Wales at Llandovery in 1799, taking advantage of the economic impact of the trade on the town to amass a personal fortune. *The Black Ox Bank,* as it was known, was eventually absorbed into *Lloyds Bank* in 1909. *Y Porthmyn*, the Welsh equivalent of *Drovers*, is also prevalent.

Druids (Derwyddon): The suffix *Druids*, a name with pre-Christian Celtic mythological connotations, is most famously associated with

Cefn Druids FC (Derwyddon Cefn), the oldest football team in Wales, formed in 1869. Johnes & Garland see the choice of name for the team as a response to nineteenth century cultural nationalism, suggesting that football also fed off the romantic nostalgia and patriotism of the period. The *Druids* is also the nickname of **Maesycwmmer FC**, a new team formed in 2010. It adopted the nickname of an earlier defunct team **Caerphilly Druids FC**, as many of the same people are involved in running the revived club. **Bangor Druids FC** competed in the North Wales Coast League in the early twentieth century. **Carmarthen Druids RFC** is the second string team of **Carmarthen Athletic RFC**. **London Welsh RFC** and **Monmouth RFC**'s second XV teams are also known as the *Druids*.

Ducks: Wattstown RFC. The origin of the nickname is attributable to a heated away match held at **Abertridwr RFC**, a neighbouring team, when fighting broke out, and several players ended up in the local river. A comment was made that the Wattstown boys 'took to the water like ducks', after which the nickname *Ducks* duly stuck.

Dynamos: Pentwyn Dynamos FC. The club, formed in 1975, play in the South Wales Senior League. The suffix *Dynamos* may owe its origins to the popularity of **FC Dynamo Moscow**, one of the most famous of all Russian football teams. The Russian club, and many other East European sporting teams take their name from the *Dinamo Sports and Fitness Club* established by the Soviets in 1923. The name given to the society was intended to imply "Power in Motion" from the Greek δύναμις; *dynamis* – power, and the Latin *motio* – motion. The term was first coined by a German inventor Ernst Werner von Siemens (1816–1892) for his revolutionary electrical generator.

Dynion Dur *see:* **Steelmen**

Dyrny: Llandyrnog United FC. *Dyrny* is an abbreviation of Llandyrnog, taken from the mutated form Teyrnog, the saint to whom the parish church is dedicated.

Eagles (Eryrod): The nickname of **Neath FC**, formed following a merger in 2005, and a team that enjoyed considerable success before winning a place in the Welsh Premier League in 2007. They were often referred to as *Yr Eryrod* in the Welsh language media. However, following some well-publicised financial problems the club was wound up in the High Court in May 2012. The club crest featured an eagle perched on a castle tower (Neath was the site of a minor Norman castle). Neighbouring **Bryn-coch RFC** are also known as the *Eagles*, and have incorporated the bird on their club emblem and match programmes.

Eithin: Cefneithin RFC. The nickname is an abbreviation of the place-name which translates as gorse *(eithin)* + ridge *(cefn)*. The club colours of green and gold hoops were chosen so as to reflect the gorse in full bloom. The club's badge also incorporates the gorse flower.

Elyrch *see:* **Swans**

Engineers: Tredomen FC. Formerly of the Welsh League, the club was nicknamed the *Engineers* after the Tredomen Engineering Works built in 1922 by the Powell Duffryn Co. and taken over in 1947 by the National Coal Board. These offices were later to become the NCB Computer Centre. The site is now part of a complex occupied by Caerphilly County Council.

Eosiaid, Yr (Nightingales): Llanybydder FC. The name *Eosiaid* and the bird's image appears on the club's crest. Attributable to their playing field which is located at Llwyn-yr-eos Farm, Alltyblaca, Ceredigion, a name that translates as 'Nightingale Bush'.

Eryrod *see:* **Eagles**

Evans Bevan Boys: Baglan Dragons FC. The team is known as the *Evans Bevan Boys*, because they play on the Evans Bevan Fields in Baglan, west of Port Talbot. The name is associated with one of the most important industrial families of South Wales who held extensive mining and brewing interests, particularly in the Vale of Neath.

Excelsiors: Excelsior is a Latin word meaning upward or progressive and has been used as a popular suffix for football teams in several countries. For example, **SBV Excelsior** is a professional football club based in Rotterdam, Netherlands. Welsh teams who have used this suffix include **Cefn Excelsiors FC**, one of the founder members of the South Wales and Monmouthshire Football Association, and **Abertillery Excelsiors FC**, who played eight seasons in the Welsh League, but who now play in the Gwent County League. The name *Excelsiors* was revived following an amalgamation of two teams, **Abertillery Town FC** and **Cwmtillery FC** to form **Tillery FC**, later re-named **Abertillery Excelsiors FC** in 2006, a suffix used by the successful **Cwmtillery Excelsiors FC** in the 1940s.

Exiles (Alltudion): *Exiles* are defined as people who have been forced to leave their native land. Following the winding up order of **Newport County FC** in 1989, it reformed and took on the name **Newport AFC**, adopting the nickname *Exiles* as a result of the need to play their first season in the Gloucestershire town of Moreton-in-Marsh due to objections from the Football Association of Wales who wished them to join the Welsh pyramid system. Eventually they won their legal battle and moved back to Wales, and in 1999 reverted to the original name of **Newport County AFC. London Welsh RFC**, recently promoted to the English Rugby Premiership are also known as the *Exiles,* as are **London Irish RFC** and **London Scottish RFC**. The Welsh equivalent, *Alltudion,* is often heard on BBC *Radio Cymru*, when discussing the fortunes of the two Welsh clubs. **Llanymynech FC** are also known as the *Exiles* as they straddle the Welsh / Shropshire border and have a good pedigree in Welsh football, having reached seven Montgomeryshire cup finals, winning on four occasions. Their playing field in actually in Shropshire, thus accounting for the *Exiles* nickname. Recently reformed in 2011, the club successfully applied to re-join the Montgomeryshire League in 2012 after plying their trade for a preparatory season in the North Shropshire Sunday League. **Wenvoe Exiles FC** compete in the Vale of Glamorgan Football League. **Rhyl Exiles RLFC** was a short-lived amateur rugby league club formed in 2010 from the disbanded **Rhyl Coasters RLFC**.

Extras: Cardiff Athletic RFC ran two teams for five seasons from

1964-65 until 1968-69, and their second XV (**Cardiff RFC's** third team) was known as the *Extras*. Similarly when **Glamorgan Wanderers RFC** ran six teams during the same decade, the fifth and sixth teams were also designated the *Extras*. An *extra* is defined as something over and above the usual required number.

Falcons: Abertysswg RFC are known as the *Falcons*. Humourously, their second XV are known as the *Pigeons,* the staple diet of the falcon. **Flintshire Falcons RLFC** are an amateur rugby league club. The name has probably been copied from the successful **Newcastle Falcons RFC** who re-branded with the bird of prey's name for the 1996–97 season.

Felin: CPD Felinheli FC. The place-name Felinheli, translates as 'tidal mill'. A water wheel is featured on the club's crest which dates the founding of the club to 1977.

Fern: Ferndale FC / Ferndale RFC. An abbreviation of the place-name.

Ferry, The: Briton Ferry Llansawel FC. A ferry to Swansea ran from the village in the fifteenth century giving its name to the village.

Fighting Irish: A nickname applied to **Aberavon Green Stars RFC**, a club founded by Irish immigrants in 1887 and drawn from the area surrounding St. Joseph's Roman Catholic Church in the Sandfields area of the town and where they found work in the booming Port Talbot iron and steel industry. The *fighting* element reflects the long struggle that the Irish have had to gain equality, and may also reflect their boisterous nature after over-indulgence in alcoholic beverages! **Aberavon Fighting Irish RLFC**, an amateur rugby league side based at the Green Stars' ground, re-branded as **Neath Port Talbot Steelers** in 2007.

Fighting Parsons: Trinity St. David's University Lampeter RFC. Rugby was first played at St. David's Theological College around 1850, and was introduced by Vice-Principal Rowland Williams (1817–70), a former Cambridge University man who was appointed to the staff in that year. This accounts for the early founding date of **Lampeter**

Town RFC, inaugural members of the Welsh Rugby Union in 1881, and a team known as the *Maroons*. However, the College teams can claim more imaginative nicknames, such as *Fighting Parsons* or *Mad Pilgrims*, which reflect the institution's history as a training college for Anglican clergymen. A team that represents former students is known as the *Old Parsonians*, playing an annual fixture against the present students.

Flower: Fleur-de-lis RFC. It is rather surprising to find a French name on a Welsh village in the heart of the Monmouthshire coalfield. Fleur-de-lys (plural: Fleurs-de-lis) is a stylized lily (in French, *fleur* means *flower*, and *lis* means *lily*) or iris that is used as a decorative design or symbol. It is well-known as the symbol of the Scout movement, and six fleur-de-lis also appear on the armorial bearings of the Kingdom of Bosnia. *Fleur de Lys* was also used as a pseudonym by the poet *Hedd Wyn* (Ellis Humphrey Evans, 1897–1917), killed in the Battle of Passchendaele shortly before he was due to be chaired at the National Eisteddfod in Birkenhead. The residents of the village of Fleur-de-lis are nicknamed *Flower* and the name has also been applied to the rugby club. Several explanations have been advanced for the origins of the name. The most credible one is given in the *Gwent village book* and links the name to religious persecution in France which forced an estimated 200,000 Protestant Huguenots to flee their country in the sixteenth and seventeenth centuries. A small group settled in this area of Wales, where they established a spelter works and a brewery, and gave the name Fleur-de-lis to their adopted community.

Foresters: Gwersyllt Foresters FC. An early football team based in the suburbs of Wrexham which competed in the inaugural Welsh Cup competition in 1877–78. The name is in all probability derived from the Ancient Order of Foresters, who had a lodge in Summerhill, Gwersyllt as early as 1873, and it is likely that some of the players were associated with the friendly society.

Foxes: Several Welsh teams carry the nickname, but for differing reasons. **Llanboidy FC** are known as the *Foxes*, in reverence to the radical landowner W. R. H. Powell MP (1819–89) of Maesgwynne, master of the Carmarthenshire hunt, and the subject of a recent biography by Dr

Denley Owen. **Leicester City FC**'s nickname also reflects that county's rich fox-hunting tradition – the outline of the county on a map is also said to resemble a fox's head. In the case of **Gwynfi United FC**, the nickname may be attributable to the surname of the Fox-Talbot land owning family of neighbouring Margam Castle. However, **Bedlinog RFC**'s nickname, is derived from the place-name, which is in all probability a combination of the Welsh *bod* (house) located near to the river *llwynog* (fox).

Ganz(i)es: A nickname recorded for **Kenfig Hill Harlequins RFC**, a breakaway team formed by the club chairman David Williams in 1931 following a rift with the secretary Will 'Rowe' Williams (*d.* 1949). Known as the *Ganzes*, they played until the outbreak of World War II. The origin of the nickname is uncertain: one theory is that local mothers used the word *gurnzeys* when telling their children to take off their jerseys. *Guernseys* and the more familiar *Jerseys* are terms for clothing which are derived from the textile industry of the Channel Islands. The Kenfig Hill *Ganz(i)es* operated until the outbreak of the Second World War in 1939. After the War, the club transferred its assets in August 1947 to old rivals **Kenfig Hill RFC.** This resulted in a Second XV being formed in season 1947–48, known as the *Cavaliers*.

Garn: An abbreviation for clubs that play in villages with the prefix *Garn,* meaning rock, such as **Garndiffaith RFC** in Torfaen and **Garnlydan FC** in neighbouring Blaenau Gwent.

Gladiators: A nickname adopted by **Glyncoch RFC**, near Pontypridd, which is probably derived from the initial two letters of the village's name. **Swansea Gladiators DRFC**, formed in 1991 are a pandisability rugby team who play their games at the home of **Swansea Uplands RFC**. A *gladiator* is a Roman swordsman who was an armed combatant entertaining audiences in violent confrontations with other gladiators, wild animals, and condemned criminals. **Swansea Gladiators DRFC** pre-dates the popular television series, *The Gladiators,* which ran from 1992 until 2000.

Glan: CPD Glantraeth FC. An abbreviated form of Glantraeth sometimes used in the local press. The Anglesey club has a ram's head as its emblem in tribute to the landowner, Mr Iolo Owen MBE, a pioneer farmer, who first developed his Easy Care Sheep in 1965 (a cross between Welsh and Wiltshire horn sheep), and who has won the champion prize at the Royal Welsh Agricultural Show on no fewer than 25 occasions. The breed requires minimal shepherding and veterinary care and yet offers excellent meat yields and high lambing ratios.

Gleision *see:* **Blues**

Goats: Llandudno RFC. The infamous wild goats of the Great Orme, the limestone head that dominates the resort of Llandudno, are featured on the club's emblem.

Gogs: RGC 1404 RFC. *Gogs*, derived from *Gog* with an English plural, is short for *Gogleddwr* or North Walian, and the nickname of **Rygbi Gogledd Cymru 1404 RFC**, a development side which has played in Division 1 East of the Welsh National League from 2012. 1404 commemorates the year that Owain Glyndŵr (c.1354–1416) was crowned Prince of Wales. **CR Caernarfon RFC**'s veteran side is also known as the *Gogs*.

Gold *see also:* **Green & Gold; Old Gold**

Goyts: Goytre United FC. An abbreviation of the name.

Graig: Pen-y-graig RFC. An abbrevation of the (g)*craig* (rock) element in the place-name. The name is originally that of a farm, later being adopted as a colliery and village name.

Gravediggers: The nickname of **Mackintosh Institute RFC**, a club which operated in the Cardiff & District Rugby Union during the early years of the twentieth century. It is uncertain why they were nicknamed the *Gravediggers,* but a possible explanation is that they may have played briefly on a recreation ground, which was then part of the land acquired and designated as a site for the expansion of a cemetery at neighbouring Cathays. As Prescott (2011) has noted: 'inevitably as the cemetery grew, the area available for recreation was gradually reduced' until the Burial

Board finally prohibited sport on that land in 1892.

Green & Ambers: Pontycymer RFC. The nickname reflects their playing colours of green and amber shirts.

Green & Blacks: Waunarlwydd RFC. The nickname reflects their playing colours of green and black hoops.

Green & Gold: Cefneithin RFC. The place-name Cefneithin translates as gorse *(eithin)* + ridge *(cefn)*. **Cefneithin RFC** will always be associated with rugby legends Carwyn James and Barry John, and the club colours of green and gold hoops reflect the gorse bush when in full bloom. The club's badge also incorporates the gorse flower.

Green & Whites: The nickname reflects the green and white playing colours of **Abertillery RFC, Caerphilly RFC** and **RTB Ebbw Vale RFC.**

Green Army: Clwb Rygbi Abergele RFC. The nickname reflects their playing colours which are primarily green. The nickname is also recorded for the **Bangor University FC**, who play in an all green kit. The traditional colours of Bangor University are green and gold.

Green Stars: Aberavon Green Stars RFC. Founded in 1887 by Irish immigrant workers which explains the team's name and playing colours of partial green shirts and green shorts, and nickname of *Fighting Irish*. The club, proud of its Welsh and Irish pedigree, still retains a strong affinity to its roots. This is reflected in the club's badge, a shield divided into quarters which represent the Irish harp and shamrock, the Prince of Wales' feathers and a red dragon. *See also:* **Stars**

Green, White & Blacks: Gwernyfed RFC, reflecting their playing colours of green shirts with a single black hoop and black shorts.

Greens: A nickname for clubs that play in green, such as **Brynaman RFC**, who play in emerald green. They first played in these colours on 6 November 1913, having previously played in blue. During their early days the team was nicknamed the **Brynaman Skullcrackers** by their fierce local rivals from **Cwmllynfell RFC. Carno FC** are also known as the *Greens*. *See also:* **Black & Green; Red & Greens**

Griffins: The nickname of **Ely Rangers FC**, founded in 1965, who are based in the western outskirts of Cardiff and play in the Welsh League. During their early days the club received considerable financial support from *Barclays Bank*, and in recognition of that support the club adopted an eagle as its symbol. *Barclays* had been famous for its iron eagle logo, used since 1690, which was considerably softened in a new design in 2007 as it was thought that the original logo had Nazi overtones and might not be attractive to Dutch customers following a bank merger. However, and somewhat ironically, the more simplistic eagle logo adopted by **Ely Rangers FC** to acknowledge their support from *Barclays* was mistaken for a *Griffin*, the logo of *Midland Bank*, and the nickname stuck. **Blackwood RFC** are also known as the *Griffins*.

Guils: Guilsfield FC. A shortened version of the place-name, possibly derived from *'Gyldi's field'*, or *gylde*, 'golden flower'.

Gunners. A nickname familiarly associated with **Arsenal FC**, whose origins can be traced to Woolwich Arsenal. The nickname has also been applied to several teams based at Royal Artillery establishments such as the short-lived **Gunners FC** of Ynys-las, Ceredigion, and more famously the **55th RA Tonfannau FC** located near Tywyn, Meirionnydd, a team that included many apprentice professional footballers among its ranks whilst engaged on their period of compulsory National Service in the 1950s. These included the late Ronnie Clayton (1934–2010) who went on to captain **Blackburn Rovers FC** and the England national team.

Gwalch: Gwalchmai FC. An abbreviation of the place-name which takes its name from Gwalchmai ap Meilir (1130–80), a medieval court poet.

Gweilch *see:* **Ospreys**

Hafod: Hafodyrynys RFC. An abbreviated form of the place-name *hafod*, meaning summer dwelling place or an area used for summer grazing. The village of Hafodyrynys in Caerphilly County Borough is a former mining village, but was once on an important droving route.

Harbourmen: Holyhead Hotspur FC. Attributable to the town's major rôle as an important harbour and ferry port. A nickname applied to the present **Holyhead Hotspur FC** team, founded in 1990, but originally associated with **Holyhead Town FC**, once a major force in Welsh football in the 1950s and 1960s. It has also been applied to **Holyhead RFC**.

Harlequins: A suffix especially popular with rugby teams describing a comic character who wore a mask and multicoloured clothes. It is generally truncated to *Quins*. *See also:* **Quins**

Harriers: Pill Harriers RFC. A team, formed in 1882, which evolved from the Pill Harriers Athletic Club, Newport. The suffix *Harriers* is popular among athletic clubs, a notable early example being **Birchfield Harriers**, formed in Birmingham in 1877. A harrier is a hound used for hunting hares, and it is believed that the use of the term *Harriers* in the world of athletics developed from a game known as *Hares & Hounds* which was prevalent in English public schools in the early nineteenth century, where "hounds" would chase "hares", the "hares" leaving paper trails in woods and hills for the hounds to pursue. A group of Londoners took up the game in 1867 as a way to keep fit and adopted the name *Harriers*. Since then, the term has become a familiar nickname for runners and their associated athletic clubs. *Harriers* was also an early nickname for **Caerphilly RFC**. A team known as **Cwm-bach Harriers FC** competed in the Aberdare Football League in the 1930s.

Hearts: Rhyl Hearts FC. A very active community club founded in 1970 whose senior side play in the Vale of Clwyd League. Influenced by the romantic name **Heart of Midlothian FC**, coupled with the fact that many Scottish players were in the **Rhyl FC** at the time, it appears that the name *Hearts* was chosen by local football activist and supporter Mr Jim Jones.

Helmets: The nickname *Helmets,* applied to the **Caerleon RFC** second XV, does not refer to rugby headgear but reflects the Roman origins of the village, and stems from the club's logo – the helmet of a Roman Centurion. The local football team, **Caerleon FC**, is known by the less imaginative name of the *Romans.*

Hen Aur *see:* **Old Gold**

Hen Blwyf, Yr *see:* **Old Parish**

Hen Ramadegwyr [Old Grammarians]: Clwb Rygbi Dolgellau RFC. The club is named after the Dolgellau County School, a grammar school established in 1665. It had a strong tradition of playing rugby.

Herbie: Herbrandston FC. A personalisation of the place-name, possibly influenced by the popularity of the *Herbie* films first released in 1968, based on the adventures of a 1963 Volkswagen Beetle.

Herrings *see:* **Penwaig**

Hibs: Cardiff Hibernian FC. The nickname is commonly adopted by teams which have an Irish immigrant connection or influence as is the case with **Hibernian FC**, the Edinburgh based Scottish Premier League club. *Hibernia* is the Latin name for Ireland, and the **Cardiff Hibernian FC**, who play in the South Wales Senior League, remain true to their tradition and play in an all green kit.

Hornets: South Wales Hornets RLFC are an amateur rugby league team based at Blackwood. **Lisvane-Heath Hornets FC** were champions in 1994 of the South Wales Senior League. *Hornets*, as in the case of **Watford FC**, usually reflects the colours found on the insect and replicated in shirts and shorts of yellow, red and black.

Hotspur: Holyhead Hotspur FC. As noted above (under **Harbourmen**), the club was founded in 1990, and probably took its name from **Tottenham Hotspur FC**, a club named in honour of Sir Henry Percy (1346–1403), whose family owned large areas of land in north

London. Sir Henry's nickname, *Harry Hotspur,* derives from his impulsive nature. Harry joined with his father and helped depose King Richard II (1367–1400) in favour of Henry of Bolingbroke, who later became King Henry IV (1367–1413).

Idris: Dolgelley Idris FC. An early football team which participated in the 1880–81 Welsh Cup competition. It took its name from the mountain, Cadair Idris, which overlooks the town. Shaped liked a chair (*cadair*), it was the seat, or fortress, of the mythological giant Idris.

Imps: Cadoxton Imps FC. A trident-carrying red *imp,* a mischievous demon in folklore, is portrayed on the badge of this Barry local football team established in 1972 by Graham Harris. They formed under the name of **Buttrills Rovers FC**, but when Cadoxton Conservative Club paid for their first kit, they changed their name to Cadoxton.

Indians: Seaside FC. The nickname *Indians* was apparently coined to frighten the opposition as they would have to enter 'dangerous Indian territory', as in Western films, if they wanted to try to ambush and defeat the Llanelli-based Carmarthenshire League team.

International: UWIC Inter Cardiff FC. Expansion of *Inter*, mimicking the famous **Inter (Internazionale) Milan FC.**

Irishmen: The nickname of **St. Paul's RFC**, a pre-Great War Cardiff & District rugby union side associated with St. Paul's Roman Catholic Church. Prescott (2011) has noted that St. Paul's were based at Newtown, one of Cardiff's earliest Irish communities, and the team were sometimes referred to as the *Irishmen* in local press reports. The team was dominated by men with Irish surnames.

Ironmen: Merthyr Tudful RFC. Attributable to the historic connection with the iron industry and a rather appropriate nickname for a rugby team.

Irons: Tredegar Ironsides RFC. Attributable to the town's long association with the iron industry. The club was founded by a group of predominantly Irish immigrants living at Iron Street, in close proximity to the iron works, which later transferred to Whiteheads, Newport.

Ironsides: Newport County FC. Formed in 1912, and as part of the build-up to **Newport County FC**'s second season, a local newspaper ran a competition to find a suitable nickname for the newcomers. The response was very positive, and eventually the name *Ironsides* was chosen, reflecting the connection that the supporters had with the iron and steel industry. The team also chose to play in black and amber stripes, mirroring the choice of colours by the town's well-established rugby club, and those of **Newport AFC** founded in 1906. As many of the workers had their roots in the English Midlands and were supporters of **Wolverhampton Wanderers FC** this seemed an appropriate choice.

Islanders: BP Barry FC. Founded in 1991, the team was based at the BP Sports and Social Club at Sully, near Barry Island.

Jackdaws: A nickname acquired by **Caerphilly AFC,** one of the Rhymney Valley's early football teams, on account of the prevalence of jackdaw nests in the walls and towers of Caerphilly's impressive Norman castle. The nickname has also been applied to **Caerphilly RFC**.

Jacks / Swansea Jack: Swansea City FC. *Jacks* has been used as a nickname for the club, for natives of Swansea, and is now commonly used as a description for the followers of **Swansea City FC**, giving rise to the popular term *Jack Army* for its supporters. *Jack Magazine* is the title of the **Swansea City FC** match day programme, and Professor Geraint Jenkins in his centenary volume has referred amusingly to a group of university lecturers known as the *Academic Jacks* (the form *Jackademics* has also been recorded by Professor Huw Bowen of Swansea University), who meet under the statue of the legendary Ivor Allchurch (1929–97) at the Liberty Stadium prior to home games. The nickname has also been adapted for Welsh language use in banners such as *Jacs y Gogledd* [North Wales Jacks]. The origins of the nickname are uncertain, but it is evident that the alias *Swansea Jack* was in use as early as 1847, when one John Griffiths, who used the alias, was charged with the death of a Cardiff man. There are two other separate instances in 1849 and 1853 of petty criminals using the alias *Swansea Jack*. *Jack*, of course, is familiar as a nickname for a sailor, and it has been suggested that *Swansea Jack* may owe its origins to the excellent reputation that Swansea's men enjoyed as skilled and dependable mariners. Another possibility is that the miners of nearby coalfields called their colleagues from Swansea by that name because their tin lunch-boxes were known as *Jacks*. The form *Jac Tun [Tin Jack]* has been recorded in a volume of mining vocabulary compiled by Lynn Davies and published in 1976. There was also a famous dog called *Swansea Jack*, a black Newfoundland retriever, who it is claimed rescued 27 people from the river Tawe during its short life of seven years from 1931 to 1937. The dog's place of burial is commemorated with a small statue on the seafront close to St. Helen's rugby ground. The dog's exploits certainly popularised the name *Swansea Jack*, and a Swansea public house, now closed, was named in his honour.

Joe's, The: St. Joseph's RFC, Cardiff. The team formed in 1959 are affectionately known as the *Joe's*.

Jolly Boys: Glan Conwy FC. Nickname of the original club formed in 1932 which folded with the advent of the Second World War. The club was reformed in 1979, and now plays in the Welsh Alliance League. The original team played in the now defunct Vale of Conwy League until the outbreak of the Second World War in 1939. They played on the Gala Field, and the carnival connotations of that name could well account for the nickname. The reformed club, who play at Cae Ffwt, have assumed the original nickname.

Keys, The: Cross Keys RFC. An industrial village which developed around an inn named the *Cross Keys*. The Welsh Premiership rugby team, officially formed in 1900, adopted the symbol of two crossed keys on its crest and became known as the *Keys*.

Kingfishers: Monmouth Town FC. The nickname reflects the club's colours of yellow shirts, with blue sleeves and blue shorts. The kingfisher is central to the club's bilingual logo, and the story is based on local folklore. Extreme local spring flooding in 1936 on the rivers Monnow and Wye effectively wiped out all of the kingfisher nests along the two rivers considered a magnet for ornithologists who came to observe this beautiful and elusive bird. Official government sources from the Ministry of Agriculture and Fisheries expressed their concern at the plight of the kingfisher population and a detailed study was commissioned to assess the damage. Amazingly the only surviving pair of breeding kingfishers were found nesting in a deflated football that had floated down the Monnow into the Wye and lodged itself with its laces in some branches overlooking the river, or so the story goes! It appears that maybe one wayward shot saved the entire population of the Wye and Monnow rivers, and at the same time gave the club its nickname of the *Kingfishers*!

Kites *see:* **Red Kites**

Klondyke: A nickname applied to the community of Dowlais and its rugby team, because of its rapid growth in the nineteeenth centuries due to the iron industry. The ensuing population explosion stands comparison with the gold rush experienced in the famous Arizona desert town of Klondyke at the beginning of the twentieth century.

Knights: The nickname of **Dowlais RFC**'s second XV.

Lakesiders: A nickname attributable to at least two mid-Wales football teams. **Bala Town FC**'s name is attributable to the proximity of *Llyn Tegid* (Bala Lake), the largest natural lake in Wales. **Bala Town FC** play at Maes Tegid – the identity of Tegid is unknown, but the name is known to date from at least the twelfth century. The Welsh word *bala* can be defined as an 'isthmus, or a route between two lakes or areas of wet ground'. Former members of the Montgomeryshire Football League **Llanwddyn FC**, founded in 1948, were also known as the *Lake, Lakesiders*, or *Lord of the Lake*. The club played their home matches at Abertrinant, close to the Lake Vyrnwy dam at Llanwddyn, built in 1881–88 to supply water to Liverpool.

Lambs: Blaina RFC: How the nickname *Lambs* was acquired is uncertain, but a sheep is included on the club's crest. Early games were played on the Mutton Tump – the origin of that name is also obscure, but the

inclusion of the element *Mutton* may account for the use of *Lambs*. *See also:*
Sheep

Latics: Aberdare Athletic FC. Formed in 1892, the Cynon Valley club graced the Football League for six seasons before they failed to gain re-election in 1927. They were known by the nickname *Latics*, a compression of the word *Athletic,* and were also referred to as the *Darians*, a name later adopted by **Aberdare Town FC**. The nickname *Latics* is more familiarly associated with **Oldham Athletic FC**, and latterly **Wigan Athletic FC**, formed in 1932, four years after the demise of **Aberdare Athletic FC.**

Laugharnees: **Laugharne RFC.**

Laughing Philosophers: The unusual nickname of **Cardiff Romilly RFC**, an early and very successful pre-Great War Canton-based Cardiff & District rugby union side. The name Romilly derives from several street names in the area associated with the estate of the John Romilly (1802–74), 1st Baron Romilly of Barry. The club used the now-demolished *Blue Anchor Inn* public house in Wharton Street, off St. Mary's Street as its headquarters, which also featured the plaster-cast figure of a laughing philosopher figure above its entrance, accounting for the nickname. It is uncertain who the figure represented but it might be the Ancient Greek philosopher Democritus, who cheerfully laughed at human follies.

Lawmen: Lex XI FC. In 1965 a group of Wrexham solicitors started playing friendly fixtures, largely for social purposes, opting to call themselves **Lex XI FC**, *lex* being Latin for law and XI the roman numerals representing eleven team players. The team eventually moved into competitive football and were inaugural members of the Cymru Alliance League. They now play in the Welsh National League (Wrexham area) and are still nicknamed the *Lawmen*.

Libs: Canton Liberals FC. A Cardiff & District Football League team founded in 2006 known as the *Libs*, operating from the Canton Liberal Club, founded in 1902.

Lido: Afan Lido FC. The Welsh Premiership Club, founded in 1967, takes its name from the Afan Lido Leisure Centre which was opened in 1965. The Lido was the site of a major fire in December 2009, and the centre has since been demolished. Plans are well advanced for its replacement.

Lilywhites: A nickname adopted by many teams who play in white shirts, notably the once mighty **Preston North End FC.** Welsh teams who have adopted the name include **Rhyl AFC** (the name appears in the publication *The colourful history of the Lilywhites*, issued in 1989), **Kenfig Hill FC** (from 1928–39), **Treharris Athletic Western FC** and **Welshpool Town FC.** *See also*: **Whites**

Limemen: Llandebie (Llandybïe) United FC. A nickname applied to a team that played in the Swansea & District League before the Great War (1914–18). The name *Limemen* was acquired because they played on a field adjacent to the impressive lime works and kilns originally built by the architect Richard Kyrke Penson (1816–86) in 1857. **Undy Athletic FC** of the Welsh League have also incorporated a lime kiln into their club badge to acknowledge the industrial past of this Gwent village.

Linnets: Barry Town FC. A nickname shared with **Kings Lynn FC** and used in the title of Jeff McInery's volume, *The Linnets – an illustrated, narrative history of Barry Town AFC,* published in 1994. The club subsequently adopted the nickname *Dragons*. In the case of **King's Lynn FC,** the name is an obvious play on the place-name *Lynn*. In Barry's case *Linnets* is thought to reflect the original green playing colours of the club, which have been revived for the 2012–13 season. Although there is no green on the *Linnet*, the closely related *Greenfinch* is also known as the *Green Linnet*.

Lions: Famously associated with the **British & Irish Lions (Llewod),** there is at least one example of its use in domestic rugby. **Llanishen RFC** are known as the *Lions,* and their crest shows a rampant silver lion, which represents the landed Lewis family of the Van, Caerphilly, who owned much of the land in Llanishen and the surrounding parishes during the sixteenth century. **CPD Penrhyn-coch FC** have also adopted the armorial bearings of a landed family, and have been called the *Lions* in local press reports, although they are more usually known by the nickname *Roosters* or the truncated *Penrhyn*. The club's emblem, which also appears on their shirts, is a black lion rampant, the family crest of the Pryse family of Gogerddan whose estate was centred on the village. The former family mansion is now part of IBERS, the University of Aberystwyth's Institute of Biological, Environmental and Rural Sciences. **Aberystwyth RFC**, who play in blue have also adopted the lion of Gogerddan as their symbol, changing its colour from the familiar black to their club colours. **Gadlys Lions FC** play in the Aberdare Valley Football League; **Marchwiel Lions FC** once played in the Clwyd League. **Mochdre Lions DFC,** a pan-disability football team, were formed in 2007.

Lizards: Lliswerry Athletic FC. Originally founded in 1926, the present reformed team dates from 1977, and play in the Gwent County League. The nickname *Lizards* is an obvious play on Lliswerry, a district of the city of Newport where *Llis* would usually be pronounced as *Lis* in this predominantly English-speaking part of Wales.

Llanbabs: A nickname for the people of Deiniolen which is sometimes applied to the local football team. It derives from the fact that many of the slate workers who came to live in Llanddeiniolen parish originated from the village of Llanbabo in Anglesey. **Deiniolen FC** folded in 2008, but has now been reformed under the name **CPD Llanbabo FC**.

Llewod *see:* **Lions**

Locos, Y: CPD Llanberis FC. The nickname *Locos* arose because the club was known as **Locomotive Llanberis FC** when it was sponsored for three seasons by the Snowdon Mountain Railway, from 1980 until 1984. Under the term of the sponsorship the club had to agree to a name change to **Locomotive Llanberis FC**. At the time the name appealed as it mirrored famous and powerful eastern European clubs such as **FC Lokomotive Leipzig** and **FC Locomotiv Moscow**. The name change proved a boon to local journalists who could have some fun with headlines such as 'Locos derailed', or 'Locos run out of steam', if they suffered an ignominious defeat. 'Locos back on track' heralded a good win!

Lord of the Lake *see:* **Lakesiders**

Machinites: Machen RFC. A early nickname recorded for the club based in Caerphilly County Borough.

Mackerel Men: New Quay FC. Derived from the town's association with mackerel fishing.

Mad Pilgrims *see:* **Fighting Parsons**

Madocians / Madocites: CPD Porthmadog FC. Two examples of early press nicknames based on the place-name derived from the founder of the town, William Alexander Maddocks (1723–1828), who enclosed a large area of marsh and built an embankment and harbour, so giving his name to the settlement.

Maglonians: Machynlleth FC. Attributed incorrectly to Maglona, which was once thought to have been the name of a Roman station on the outskirts of the town, a theory now discounted by historians. *The Maglonians* was used as the title of the club's centenary volume by David Wyn Davies, published in 1985.

Magpies (Piod): Famously the nickname of **Newcastle United FC, Notts County FC** and many other clubs who play in black and white striped shirts. Several clubs in Wales are also known by the same name, and for the same reason. These include **Barmouth & Dyffryn United FC**, whose club emblem depicts a magpie standing on a football, **Bow Street FC**, who have also named their ground *Cae Piod* [Field of the Magpie], and include the bird as a central feature on the club's crest. **Cardigan Town FC, Lampeter Town FC, Garden Village FC, Llanfyllin Town FC** and **Pembroke Borough FC** are among other teams who carry the nickname. Some rugby teams have also acquired the name: **Tumble RFC** play in black and white hooped shirts, and their club crest shows a magpie and daffodil above the wording 'Clwb Rygbi

Y Tymbl'. **Vardre RFC**, of the Swansea Valley, with a club crest show-
ing two magpies, also play in black and white hoops, and they, like **Bow
Street FC**, have named their playing field Maes-y-bioden [Field of the
Magpie].

Major, The: Llantwit Major FC. *The Major*, an abbreviated version
of the place-name, is the nickname of the club and the title of its matchday programme.

Marauders: Montgomeryshire Marauders RLFC. A short-lived
amateur rugby league team based at Welshpool.

Margarines: Glyn-neath RFC. Early supporters were often heard to
shout 'Up the *Margarines*', which according to an old Glyn-neath stal-
wart, quoted in *Welsh Rugby* in August 1972, originated from the fact that
in those early days 'it was very difficult to scrape a side together'!

Mariners: Milford Haven RFC. The nickname derives from its fine
natural harbour and maritime tradition which has seen the town develop
into a significant sea port and oil and gas terminal. The club play on the
Observatory Field so named after Charles Francis Greville (1749–1809)
who established an astronomical observatory on the estuary.

Maroons: Lampeter Town RFC. Formed in 1881, **Lampeter
Town RFC** are known as the *Maroons* due to their shirt colours and were
founder members of the Welsh Rugby Union. Rugby came early to the
town and was probably first played at St. David's Theological College,
Lampeter, around 1850, after being introduced by Vice-Principal Rowland Williams (1817–70), a former Cambridge University student, following his appointment to the staff in that year.

Martyrs: Merthyr Town (Tydfil) FC. Derived from the place-name
which is based on the martyrdom of Tudful, one of the many daughters
of the legendary Brychan Brycheiniog, fifth-century king of Brycheiniog,
and father of 46 children from three wives. The element *merthyr* is Welsh
for *martyr*.

Meds: Cardiff Medicals RFC. A university team with an 80-year-old tradition currently fielding a number of sides drawn from medical, dentistry, nursing and physiotherapy students at Cardiff.

Meibion y Daran *see:* **Darans**

Men of Preseli / Preselimen: Clwb Rygbi Crymych RFC. A village located in the shadow of the Preseli Hills in north Pembrokeshire.

Men of the Mawr: Bryn-mawr RFC. An earlier nickname for the team was *City of the Hills Boys.*

Met: An abbreviation for the rugby and football teams fielded by Cardiff Metropolitan University.

Mighty Bryn: Brynithel RFC.

Mighty Quins: Aberavon Quins RFC.

Milkmen: Felin-fach CPD / FC: Known as the *Milkmen* due to the presence of a creamery in the village which closed in 1986, but which has since been used for the production of allied products. The club badge incorporates a windmill, although the village derives its name from a water mill, smaller than Llanllŷr's less than a mile to the east, and hence the name Felin-fach, or 'little mill'.

Millers: The nickname of **Newcastle AFC**, a Shropshire club based at Newcastle-on-Clun, who play in the Mid-Wales League (South). In the same way as **Rotherham United FC**, also known as the *Millers*, the Shropshire club's nickname is derived from their home ground, Mill Field, which is located close to a Grade II listed water mill dating from the eighteenth century. Although Rotherham have since 2008 vacated their traditional home at Millmoor, a ground built on the site of a flour mill, for a new stadium, they are still known as the *Millers*.

Miner Birds: Penallta Miner Birds LRFC are a ladies' rugby team operating from **Penallta RFC**. *See also:* **Pitmen**

Miners: Swansea Valley Miners RLFC. An amateur rugby league team formed in 2004, who developed from the **Swansea Bulls RLFC**, formed in 2002. Initially they played at Morriston before relocating to Ystalyfera.

Mission: Bridgend Street FC. Bridgend Street was a residential street in the Splott district of Cardiff. It was situated off Portmanmoor Road, a vibrant area, full of shops, public houses, off licences and houses. In 1973 the decision was made to demolish many buildings as part of the City Council's regeneration programme. Hundreds of houses were pulled down, destroying a very close knit community, and Bridgend Street was one of the affected streets. The street included a mission hall called Bridgend Street Mission which was an outlet for many activities and sporting ventures, including **Bridgend Street FC** founded in 1899. However, the team's nickname, the *Mission*, lives on.

Mount: Mountain Ash RFC are known as the *Mount* in addition to their more traditional nickname of *Old Firm*.

Mountain Men: A nickname shared by **Flint Mountain FC**, a village located on a hill south-west of Flint and **Garw Athletic FC**, which reflects the fact that the club is based in the upper reaches of the Garw Valley at Pontycymer, near Bridgend.

Mourners: *see:* **All Blacks**

Mules: Kenfig Hill RFC. The nickname *Mules* apparently dates from the pre-World War II period of legendary honorary secretary and former player Will "Rowe" Williams (*d.* 1949). He was secretary of the club from 1917 until 1934, and was one of the club's severest touchline critics. A shopkeeper by trade he was a familiar figure in the village with his ice-cream cart; he later became a publican at the *Walnut Tree* in Kenfig Hill. In a match played at **Glyncorrwg RFC** in the early 1920s, he grew increasingly frustrated with Kenfig's constant kicking game, which usually ended with the ball landing in the nearby river Corrwg. When he started shouting 'You're just like a bunch of bloody *mules*. Stop fly-kicking the damn ball, and try running with it for a change', the name stuck, and was adopted as the club's nickname and incorporated into its crest. It was said that when the team went to play their away games, the local children would shout in Welsh – 'Mae'r Mulod yn dod'. [The *Mules* are coming].

Mushroooms / Mush: Mid Rhondda FC. Martin Johnes has explained that the nickname *Mushrooms* was earned by the Tonypandy based team because it provided an image of rapid growth, indicating that the team had risen virtually over-night when it was established in 1912, mirroring the industrial development of the Rhondda Valleys. **Mid-Rhondda FC** folded in 1928. *Mushrooms* is sometimes abbreviated to *Mush,* as in the case of **Abercwmboi Mush FC** who entered the Aberdare Valley Football League in 1924.

Musselmen: Conwy Borough FC. The nickname reflects the importance of musseling in the town since Roman times, and it is still carried out today in the same traditional way. Conwy has a popular musseling museum on its quayside which is a major tourist attraction.

Nanty: Nantyffyllon RFC. An abbreviation of the place-name and the club's modern nickname, replacing the *Reds,* first adopted in the 1930s, but abandoned once the club's shirt colours were changed to green and red. The club's crest incorporates an interesting feature – the *Garnwen Beacon,* amusingly called 'the pineapple'. It symbolizes a beacon lit in bye gone days to warn residents of the Llyfni Valley of a possible attack by foreigners.

Newts: New Tredegar RFC. A relatively new club formed in 1977 – the nickname is a plural combination of *New* and *T* in New Tredegar.

Nightingales *see:* **Eosiaid, Yr**

Nomads. A nickname originally adopted by teams that found difficulty in locating a permanent home playing field. Several clubs in Wales carry the name including **Gap Connah's Quay FC** (formerly known as **Connah's Quay Nomads FC**), **FC Nomads** (of Connah's Quay, a new club formed in 2009 'to protect football in Connah's Quay follow-

ing the merger plans of Gap Connah's Quay and Flint Town United'),
Holt Nomads FC and **Neyland FC**. In Connah's Quay's case, the suffix *Nomads* was apparently chosen in 1946 by the club chairman because the club was always being drawn away at distant venues in south Wales when they entered the Welsh Amateur Cup! The Swansea Senior League side **Hafod Brotherhood FC** would change their name to **Swansea Nomads FC** when touring England and the Continent during the postwar era.

'Nops: Caernarfon (Carnarvon) Ironopolis FC. An abbreviation of the name of the early football team formed in 1895, that reached the semi-final of the Welsh Cup in 1902, before folding in 1903. Known as the *Canaries* because of their association with the town, they were the works team of the De Winton & Co. iron works which at its zenith employed 180 men in its premises on the quayside at Caernarfon. The football team was established by Parry Jones, son of an Anglesey vicar, a football enthusiast, and one of the senior managers at the works. *See also:* **Canaries**

Normalites: A familiar name used to describe students of Bangor Normal Teachers' Training College and which was also applied to their rugby and football teams. The college, established in 1861, merged with Bangor University in 1996. The name is derived from the French colleges known as *écoles normale*, the earliest of which was established in Reims in 1685. They were founded to train schoolteachers, and sought to 'normalise' educational standards.

North: Llandaff North RFC. The abbreviated name *North* is used as a nickname. Players who joined the club were amusingly often recorded as having 'gone north', an euphemism for defecting to rugby league.

North End: Bangor North End FC, a club formed in the 1890s, taking its name in all probability from **Preston North End FC**.

O's: Overton Recreational FC. An initialism possibly influenced by the nickname of **Leyton Orient FC**, who are also known as the *O's*.

Oilmen: BP Llandarcy FC / RFC. Named after the works teams associated with the Anglo-Persian Oil Company refinery opened in 1922 at Llandarcy, near Neath, which later became part of the British Petroleum global conglomerate. **BP Llandarcy FC** played in the Welsh League from 1971 until 1999.

Old Firm: Mountain Ash RFC. A nickname famously associated with the rivalry between Glasgow **Rangers FC** and Glasgow **Celtic FC**. The origin of the term is unclear but may derive from the commercial benefits of the two clubs' rivalries. Its application to **Mountain Ash RFC** probably refers to the early foundation of the club in 1875. The club website records that the name was popularised by a hawker named Mr Wiltshire who used to frequent home matches and would shout "the old firm, the old firm, patronise the old firm" when selling his fruit produce to spectators. It is believed that the name was popularised by the original 'Old Stager' (J. R. Stephens), a *Western Mail* journalist, who reported on matches during the last decade of the nineteenth century. Although the nickname *Old Firm* for **Mountain Ash RFC** is first recorded in the *Western Mail* on 21 November 1898, 'Old Stager' is not used as a pseudonym until after 1900. However, the pen-name is most famously associated with the journalist W. J. Hoare who wrote for the same newspaper in the 1920s and 1930s.

Old Gold (Yr Hen Aur): Carmarthen Town FC. The Welsh Premiership football club are known as the *Old Gold*, and have played in old gold shirts and black shorts since their formation in 1950. The choice of colours was apparently made by the late John 'Jack' Miles Harding (1894–1976), prime mover in the founding of the club, and the colours were chosen because they reflected those worn by one of the most successful teams of the day, **Wolverhampton Wanderers FC**. However, Jack Harding was a native of South Shields, Co. Durham, and not a natural Wolves supporter. *Yr Hen Aur* has become a familiar Welsh translation of the nickname.

Old Grammarians *see:* **Hen Ramadegwyr**

Old Parish (Yr Hen Blwyf): Maesteg RFC. *Old Parish* refers to

Llangynwyd parish which includes the modern settlement of Maesteg. There are several versions of how the name *Old Parish* was acquired. One dubious but interesting explanation relates to the burial of a young man who died at the age of 28 years. The carpenter, an apprentice, who prepared his coffin did not know how to write 28, but remembered that four 7s would equate to that age, and carved 7777 on the coffin. The visiting pastor, who took the funeral, enquired 'How long has this man lived in the parish?' and was told in reply 'All his life'. The vicar replied ' This must be a very old parish', and the name has stuck ever since, and has been adopted as the nickname of **Maesteg RFC**! The 7777 also appears prominently on the club's emblem.

Old Parsonians *see:* **Fighting Parsons**

Olympic: A suffix applied to **Wrexham Olympic FC**, formed in 1883, after **Wrexham FC** was disbanded for crowd trouble. The club reverted to its former name within three years. The choice of suffix was influenced by the success of **Blackburn Olympic FC** (1878–89), and predates the establishment of the modern Olympic Games in 1896. The suffix lives on in the name of **Morriston Olympic FC**, of the Swansea Senior Football League.

Orkeis / Orkyites: An early nickname for **Treorchy RFC** when the common spelling of the town was Treorky.

Ospreys (Gweilch): The name adopted for the professional regional rugby side formed in 2003 from the merger of **Neath RFC** and **Swansea RFC**. They share the Liberty Stadium with **Swansea City FC**. The name *Ospreys* was chosen as the bird of prey already appeared on the **Swansea RFC** centenary logo issued in 1973. The current logo of the team also displays an Osprey mask.

Otters: Narberth RFC. Formed in 1879, the club play at the Lewis Lloyd Ground in the Pembrokeshire town. The field, originally known as Bloomfield Meadow was given as an outright gift to the club in 1945 by Miss Lewis Lloyd, an enthusiastic supporter of the local otter hunt. The field was officially opened on 16 September 1948 and re-named the

Lloyd Lewis Ground in recognition of her generosity. In 1965 the club adopted the otter as its emblem to further acknowledge Miss Lloyd's gift, giving rise to the club's nickname *Otters*. The club's emblem, which shows an otter sitting on top of a shield, has also been adopted by **Narberth RFC**, an American High School, in Pennsylvania, USA.

Owls: Brynithel RFC. The club was formed in 1975, and were subject to many severe losses averaging over 50 points a game during their first season. Apparently, one local, and a non-rugby supporter, enquired one evening at their traditional watering hole how the team had performed, and was told by a group of the players that they had again lost by over 60 points. Hardly surprised to hear the news, the local attributed the heavy losses to the team's overindulgence in the alcoholic beverage, stating that the players were intoxicated like owls, or words to that effect! Following that comment, the badge of an owl was introduced, and the nickname was adopted.

Panthers: Welsh teams with the *Panthers* suffix, a large cat, include **Prestatyn & Rhyl Panthers RLFC** and **Swansea Panthers FC**, a Swansea Senior League side with a panther logo created by Eifion Kaine. **Pembrokeshire Panthers RLFC** competed for one season in the Rugby League Welsh Conference (West) in 2006.

Park: Maesteg Park FC. The former League of Wales team was nicknamed *The Park*. The Club was dissolved in 2010.

Pembrokeshire Scarlets *see:* **Scarlets**

Penmen: Penmaen-mawr FC. The nickname of a team that played in the Welsh League (North) from 1939 until 1975.

Pennies: Abergavenny Thursdays FC. This Monmouthshire club with an illustrious history is known by several nicknames, including the *Pennies,* attributable to the location of the club's ground in the Pen-y-pound district of the town. Abergavenny is also Cockney rhyming slang for *pennies*.

Penrhyn: CPD Penrhyn-coch FC. An abbreviation of Penrhyn-coch.

Penwaig [Herrings]: Nefyn United FC. The sea has always provided an important livelihood for the residents of the Llŷn peninsula, and fishing for herring (*penwaig*) was particularly lucrative as indicated by the presence of three herrings on the town's coat of arms. In 1635 the vast majority of Nefyn's male population of 60 worked as fishermen, and in 1771 the annual herring catch was valued at over £4,000. By the beginning of the twentieth century over 40 Nefyn boats were connected to the herring fishing industry, but the industry largely collapsed after the Great War. However, the name *Penwaig Nefyn* has retained its usage and three herrings and two footballs appear on the club's bilingual crest.

Pesda: Bethesda Athletic FC / Clwb Rygbi Bethesda. *Pesda* is a colloquial name for Bethesda.

Phoenix: The symbol of rebirth and renewal based on the Greek mythological bird. A name applied to **Phoenix Wanderers FC** of Pontypool, one of the earliest team in Wales and founder members of the South Wales League in 1890. A phoenix appears on the club crest of **Penmaen-mawr Phoenix FC**, a team formed after the demise of **Penmaen-mawr FC** who played in the Welsh League (North) from 1939 until 1975. A university students' team named **Phoenix FC** graced the Aberystwyth & District Football League with relative success for over 20 seasons from 1969 to 1993, winning the championship title in 1972–73 (they were reformed in 2008 under the name **FC Phoenix**). **Treharris Phoenix RFC** was established in 2009, seven years after the collapse of **Treharris RFC**, and also has a phoenix on its club badge. **Pen-coed Phoenix LRFC** is a ladies' rugby team.

Picwn *see:* **Wasps**

Pigeons: Abertysswg Falcons RFC's second XV are called the *Pigeons*, the staple diet of the bird of prey!

PILCS FC: Strictly an acronym rather than a nickname for **Pontyfelin**

Institute for Leisure, Culture and Sport, a Gwent County Football League team originally formed in 1952 as the works team of the glass manufacturers Pilkington who established a factory at Pontyfelin, near Pontypool in 1952.

Piod *see:* **Magpies**

Pirates: South Wales Pirates DRFC. The *Pirates* are a regional wheelchair rugby team based at Cardiff. The name was probably chosen to pay homage to Cardiff's maritime tradition, in similar vein to the **Cornish Pirates RFC**, the West Country Championship side.

Pitmen: A nickname associated with mining towns and villages. **Tonmawr RFC** owes its origins and nickname to the traditional industry of this Vale of Neath community. **Penallta RFC**, founded by a group of miners in 1952, are also known by the name *Pitmen*, and although the colliery closed in 1992 the Ystrad Mynach club still continues to play under its name. Their ladies' team is known as **Penallta Miner Birds RFC**. **Trefonen FC**, based in Shropshire, and who play in the Montgomeryshire League, are another team known as the *Pitmen*. They play their matches on a public playing field, known locally as the *Pit,* owing to its proximity to an old coal mine. Mining was carried out in the village from the early eighteenth century until 1891.

Planemakers: Airbus Broughton UK FC. The Welsh Premiership football team which has its origins as a works-based team at the British aerospace factory in Broughton, Flintshire was once generally known as the *Planemakers*. As the factory has now specialised in the production of aeroplane wings the team is generally known by its more modern nickname of *Wingmakers*.

Pont / Ponty: An abbreviation used for place-names which include the element *pont (bridge)*. **Pontlottyn AFC**, formed in 2008, and now of the South Wales Senior League are known as *Pont,* whereas **Pontardawe RFC, Pontypridd FC** and **Pontypridd RFC** are known as *Ponty. See also:* **Bont; Bridge**

'Pool: A common nickname for football and rugby teams based at Welshpool. The town was known as *Pool* until the fifteenth century.

Pooler: Pontypool RFC. A familiar nickname for this famous club which produced the legendary Pontypool front row of the 1970s and 1980s, immortalised in song by entertainer Max Boyce. The place-name *Pont y poole* was recorded as early as 1614; C. J. O. Evans mentions that the settlement was known as *Le Pool* in the thirteenth century.

Port: CPD Porthmadog FC. Owen & Morgan note that 'although Portmadoc has been supplanted by Porthmadog, the town in colloquial local usage is still frequently referred to as *Port*', a nickname which also applies to the football team.

Porthmyn *see:* **Drovers**

Premiers: An early nickname for **Caerphilly RFC.**

Preselimen *see:* **Men of Preseli**

Pride of the Seaside: Sea View RFC. The Barry based club, formed in 2008, is the newest rugby club in Wales.

Pumas: Pontprennau Pumas FC. The *Pumas* compete in the Cardiff Combination Football League. The puma, a large cat, is most famously associated with *Los Pumas*, nickname of the Argentine rugby team.

Quarrymen: A nickname applied to both football and rugby teams from the slate mining areas of north Wales such as **Blaenau** (Ffestiniog) **Amateurs FC** and **CR Bro Ffestiniog RFC. Blaenau Amateurs FC** also has a slate wagon depicted on its club's crest.

Quays: New Quay FC. An abbreviation of the place-name which has been used when referring to the club in local newspaper press reports.

Quins: An abbreviation of *Harlequins*. Adopted as the nickname of rugby teams **Aberavon Quins RFC** (also known as the *Mighty Quins*), **Cardiff**

Harlequins (formerly **Cardiff High School Old Boys RFC**), **Maesteg Harlequins RFC**, **Pembroke Dock Harlequins RFC** and **Porth Harlequins RFC**. **Tenby Harlequins RFC** merged with **Tenby Swifts RFC** in 1901 to form **Tenby United RFC**. Football team **Cardiff Grange Harlequins FC** are also known as the *Quins*.

Radicals: Llanelli Radicals FC. The club was formed in 1986 as **Nuffield Rangers FC** changing its name to **Llanelli Radiators FC** in 1987 to acknowledge the firm's generosity in allowing what was at the time a junior side to play on land adjacent to the factory. After the company became part of the Japanese Calsonic Kansei Corporation, the team name again changed to **Calsonic FC**. In 2002 a senior side was formed for the first time to compete in the Carmarthenshire League and was named **Llanelli Radicals FC**, cleverly combining the two elements of *radiators* and *calsonic* found in the previous names. **Llanelli Radicals FC** senior team has now folded, but **Calsonic Kansei Swiss Valley FC** are still going strong.

Radnor Robins: Knighton Town FC. The nickname reflects their playing colours of red shirts and white shorts.

Rads: Morriston Olympic FC. 'The Rads' derives from the early sponsorship of the club by Carmarthen-based Olympic Radiators.

Rags / Rags & Tatters: The nickname of **Cardiff Athletic RFC**, the second XV of **Cardiff RFC**. Established in 1880, four seasons after the establishment of the club, they were re-named **Cardiff Athletic RFC** in 1931–32. The nickname *Rags* dates from that period, and was probably bestowed by Sydney Charles Cravos (1903–59), who captained the Second XV in 1925–26, playing on until the 1930s. During the 1960s the **Athletic** ran a second string for five seasons known as the *Tatters* or *Extras*.

Raiders: Wrexham Bradley Raiders RLFC. The *Raiders* are an amateur rugby league club, a name probably influenced by the famous Australian team, **Canberra Raiders RLFC**.

Railwaymen: The nickname famously applied to **Crewe Alexandra FC** was shared by **Llandudno Junction FC**, who amalgamated in 1954 with their great rivals **Conwy Borough FC** to form **Borough United FC**, a short-lived team that won overnight fame when it won the Welsh Cup in 1963 and competed in the European Cup Winners Cup. **Borough United FC** folded in 1969.

Rangers: A suffix chiefly associated with Glasgow **Rangers FC**, formed in 1872, and a name apparently copied from an English rugby team after it was found in an annual publication. Several Welsh teams that have adopted the name include the Carmarthenshire based Ceredigion League side **Bargod Rangers FC**, **Bwlch Rangers FC** of the Carmarthenshire League, together with **Brickfield Rangers FC** and **Hawarden Rangers FC**, both of whom play in the Welsh National League (Wrexham Area).

Ravens: *Ravens* is the traditional nickname of **Bridgend RFC** and the team is now known as **Bridgend Ravens RFC**. A raven also features prominently on the emblem of **Cogan Coronation FC** and **Dinas Powys FC**, and the latter club once published a fanzine entitled *Raven Loonies*. **Sea View Ravens RFC**, a successful ladies' rugby team, are based in Barry. The adoption of the nickname *Ravens* in all these instances is due to the association of the Irish family of the earl of Dunraven who once held considerable landed interests in Glamorgan. A raven features prominently on the coat of arms of Bridgend Town Council.

Ravers: Roath Ravers FC. Following a rare gaffe by Jeff Stelling on Sky Sports Soccer Special on 5 March 2011, when **Raith Rovers FC** scored a second goal in their match against **Queen of the South FC**, he mistakenly announced that 'it could be a very good day indeed for **Roath Ravers**'. The spoonerism became a You Tube hit, and the name **Roath Ravers FC** was subsequently adopted by a five-a-side team from the Roath area of Cardiff playing in the local Thursday league.

Rebels: Fairwater Rebels FC. The *Rebels* play in the Cardiff Combination League. **Glyncorrwg RFC**'s second XV are also known as the *Rebels*.

Red & Blacks: Carmarthen Athletic RFC. The nickname is attributable to their club colours of red & black hooped jerseys, black shorts, and black socks with red tops.

Red & Greens: Merthyr Town FC. The nickname reflected their playing colours of red and green.

Red & Whites: Newcastle Emlyn RFC and **Oakdale RFC.** The nickname reflects the colours of red & white hooped shirts worn by both clubs.

Red Army: An alternative nickname once used for **Wrexham FC**, and a name drawn from the Soviet Union's national army.

Red Devils: When the Belgium national football team became the first continental side to visit Wales in 1949, losing 5–1, Phil Stead records that the Cardiff City Chairman, Herbert Merrett, asserted Wales' right to take on the traditional nickname of the opponents. He wrote: "The Welshmen as the home team wear the traditional red shirts and will take on the pseudonym of the *Red Devils'*. The Belgian team still carry the nickname which is also famously associated with **Manchester United FC**. See also: **Devils**

Red Dragons (Dreigiau Cochion): A nickname applied to the **Wales** national football and rugby teams (and used recently as the title of Phil Stead's history of Welsh football), **Wrexham FC** (from 2001) and the re-branded **Cardiff City FC**, following their controversial change in 2012 from their traditional blue to the red shirts favoured by their Malaysian owners who consider the colour a more dynamic choice in terms of marketing in Asia. *See also:* **Dragons**

Red Kites: Rhayader Town FC. A nickname which appears to have been adopted by the reformed club which came into existence in 2007, although the traditional nickname of *Thin Red Line* is still in use. The Red Kite also features prominently on the club's badge. The nickname is derived from the majestic bird of prey, revived successfully from the brink of extinction, which is now a common sight in this area. Gigrin

Farm Feeding Station on the outskirts of the town provides an opportunity to see these impressive creatures at very close hand.

Redbirds: Cardiff City FC. A new nickname coined by the press after their controversial re-branding. *Adar Gleision Coch* [Red Bluebirds] has also been used in the Welsh language press.

Reds (Cochion): A nickname applied to teams who play in red shirts. These include **Corwen FC, Cwmavon RFC, Kenfig Hill FC** (founder members of the Port Talbot & District Football League in 1926), **Llanelli FC, Newcastle Emlyn FC, Pencader FC, Pen-clawdd RFC** and **Wrexham FC**. In **Pen-clawdd**'s case, although they also play in red, the reason for their famous battle cry 'Up the *Reds*' is a little different. It is thought that the name originated during the period leading up to the Great War when the club's shrewd secretary, Frank Lewis, succeeded in pulling the club out of its precarious financial 'red' position. The nickname *Reds* was thereafter adopted as a term of endearment for the club, and a constant reminder of the past lean times. **Nantyffyllon RFC** were also one known as the *Reds* due to their playing colours but which were later changed. *See also:* **Super Reds**

Refresh: Abercregan Refresh FC. The club played in the Port Talbot Football League until it folded in 2009, and took its unusual name from the *Refreshment Rooms,* a public house based in the preserved Great Western Railway Station.

Rhiewsiders: Berriew FC. The Powys village takes its name from the mouth (*aber*) of the river Rhiw. The nickname *Rhiewsiders* is well-established.

Rhinos: The suffix *Rhinos* was adopted by **Leeds Rhinos RLFC** in 1997 and seems to have been copied by several Welsh teams. These include **Llantwit Fardre RFC, Rumney Rhinos RLFC**, a short lived rugby league team, originally formed in 2003, evolving in 2004 to the **Titans RLFC** (formerly **Newport Titans RLFC**), and the **Amman Valley Rhinos RLFC** who competed for one season in 2010. **Rumney RFC**'s second XV are also known as the *Rhinos*. The rhino, an abbreviation of rhinoceros, is an aggressive charging beast, and its general prowess makes it a suitable choice of suffix for a rugby team.

Rhondda Bulldogs *see:* **Bulldogs**

Rhondda Zebras *see:* **Zebras**

Rhyfelwyr *see:* **Warriors**

Riders: Cefn Cribwr RFC. A nickname derived from the exploits of a band of robbers known as the *Cefn Riders* who roamed the area in the mid fifteenth century. It appears that they were based in the Lordship of Brecon, but frequently raided deep into villages of the Lordship of Ogmore including Cefn Cribwr. They were known as the *Riders* owing to their peculiar habit of forcing their victims to carry them the length of the village, or face the inevitable consequences of refusal.

Riverboaters: Caerau Athletic FC. The **Caerau Athletic FC** Social Club, the Riverboat Club, has given rise to this nickname.

Riversiders: Kenfig Hill FC, reformed in 1945, were known briefly as **Kenfig Hill Riversiders FC,** until the suffix was dropped in 1952. **Robins (Robiniaid).** A popular nickname usually associated with teams who play in red and white, such as **Bristol City FC** and **Charlton Athletic FC.** Welsh teams known as the *Robins* include **Milford United FC, Newtown FC** (who also have *Rocky the Robin* as their mascot), **Pennar Robins FC, Ton-du Robins** and **Wrexham FC**, for which the Welsh form *Robiniaid* has also been recorded. Although **Wrexham FC**'s traditional colours are red and white, the nickname *Robins* actually derives from the long serving secretary and manager Ted Robinson who was in post from 1907 to 1924. **Knighton FC** are known as the *Radnor Robins*. Rugby teams sharing the nickname *Robins* include **Birchgrove RFC.**

Rockets: An early nickname for **Aber-porth FC** derived from the presence of the Royal Aircraft Establishment (RAE) in this Ceredigion coastal town. As a missile testing station, the team was affectionately known as the *Rockets*. The modern preferred nickname appears to be the *Airmen*. During their early years **Dafen Welfare FC**, near Llanelli, were also known as the *Rockets*. It would seem unlikely that the name has a connection with the military range established at Pembrey Sands some 8 miles west of Dafen.

Rocks: St. Peter's RFC. Known as the *Rocks*, St. Peter's is a rugby club based in the Roath area of Cardiff and was originally founded to provide recreation for the growing Roman Catholic population. The nickname has Biblical origins from the Gospel according to St. Matthew, chapter 16.18 when Jesus uttered to Peter 'You are Peter, the Rock; and on this rock I will build my church'. The nickname appears in the title of the centenary volume *One hundred years of the 'Rocks'*, by Des Childs, published in 1986. As with the Vatican's coat of arms, the metaphorical keys of the Kingdom of Heaven appear on the club's emblem.

Rogie Aces: Rogerstone FC. A nickname used by the supporters of **Rogerstone FC** who play in the Gwent Football League. *Rogie,* an abbrevation of Rogerstone, is also applicable to **Rogerstone RFC**. It is believed that the nickname *Aces* derives from a nineteenth century Geordie folk song entitled *Blaydon Races* which has been adapted for local use by several clubs. The Rogestone version goes as follows:

> "Ohhhhhh the lads, you ought to şee us coming,
> Fastest team in the land you ought to see us running,
> All the lads and lasses with smiles upon their faces,
> Walking down the Risca road
> To see the Rogie Aces."

Romans: The predictable nickname of **Caerleon FC** which is based in the former Roman stronghold. The club's crest depicts the Roman legionary fortress at Caerleon, and the team's home ground, Cold Bath Road, has Roman origins and is located close to several architectural remains from that period. The local rugby club's Second XV has a more creative nickname in *Helmets*. **Merthyr Town FC** were also known as the *Romans* during their early days as their ground Penydarren Park was built on the site of a Roman fort. The Roman presence at Merthyr was first discovered in 1786 during the building of Penydarren House for the ironmaster Samuel Homfray (1762–1822).

Rooks: Carew FC. The nickname is attributable to the presence of nesting rooks in the walls of Carew Castle, the impressive Pembrokeshire fortress. The nickname *Rooks* is shared with **Carew Hockey Club**, and appears on their emblem as well as that of the **Carew Cricket and Football Club.** Two rooks also feature on the emblem of **Trebanos RFC.**

Roosters: CPD Penrhyn-coch FC. The nickname *Roosters* is now used on the club's matchday programmes, official website and club shirts, although the origins of the name are unclear. What is certain is that it is a relatively new nickname, first recorded in 1998, and officially adopted on the club's programme during the 2007–08 season. It has been suggested that it may have stemmed from one of the players, while others have contended that it may have originated in press reports published in the Montgomeryshire *County Times*. However, a search of the paper during this period appears to suggest that *Lions* was the preferred nickname at the time. It seems likely, however, that the nickname has something to do with the name Penrhyn-coch, and its association with the colour red *(coch)*, which is reflected in the club's first choice colours of red and black. According to Iwan Wmffre, *coch* in Penrhyn-coch probably refers to 'vegetation such as fern, or perhaps shallow soil that withers earlier in dry-periods'. The club colour black comes from the black lion rampant of Gogerddan, the club's emblem, which it could be argued is not too dissimilar to a cockerel! It has also been suggested that the name *Roosters* may have emanated from the fact that *Penrhyn* were a very strong home side, seldom losing, and a team happiest when 'roosting at home'! The fact that the song *Little Red Rooster* sung by the *Rolling Stones* reached number one in the UK charts in December 1964, shortly before **Penrhyn-coch FC** was established in 1965, does not appear to be an influencing factor in the choice of this nickname, as the name was unknown to those who played for the club during the late 1960s and 1970s. *See also:* **Rwsters**

Rovers: A common suffix similar in its meaning to *Wanderers*, suggesting a team of roving warriors, and sometimes indicating a homeless team at its outset. Famous examples are **Blackburn Rovers FC, Bristol Rovers FC, Raith Rovers FC** and the fictional **Melchester Rovers FC** with its star striker Roy Race (Roy of the Rovers). **Westminster Rovers FC** were an early team based in the Wrexham area. Today, Welsh teams who carry the suffix include **Albion Rovers FC, Tynte Rovers FC** (once of the Welsh League) and Welshpool's **Waterloo Rovers FC**. A popular suffix in English rugby league circles, its use in rugby union in Wales is hardly evident. However, **Maesteg Rovers RFC** were an early team in the Llyfni Valley.

Royal Stars: Cwm-bach Royal Stars FC *see also:* **Stars**

Royals: Reading FC carry the nickname *Royals* due to their location in the Royal county of Berkshire. Similarly, the nickname *Royals* for **Talgarth Town FC** is derived from the fact that Talgarth was once the royal residence of the legendary Brychan, King of Brycheiniog in the fifth century AD. With three wives, 24 daughters, and 22 sons the family was an important force in Wales at that time. Responsible for the spread of Christianity throughout Brycheiniog, the daughters of Brychan and their descendants account for almost all of the saints of south Wales and include the grandmother of patron saint St. David. **Treorchy RFC** played in royal blue for their first three seasons and were also known as the *Royals*, or *Royal Boys of Treorky*. They changed to their familiar black and white hooped shirts in 1889. **The Royal Regiment of Wales XV**, who compete in the Army Cup, are another example of a team that has adopted the nickname.

'Rug: Llanrug United FC. An abbreviation of the mutated element *(g)rug,* meaning heather.

Ruthinites / Ruthless / Ruths: Ruthin Town FC. The three nicknames are all a play on the place-name.

Rwsters: Llanrwst United FC. The nickname *Rwsters* [*Roosters*] is a play on *Gw(rwst)*, the second and personal name element of the place-name. *See also:* **Roosters**

Saints (Seintiau): A nickname often, but not always, associated with place-names that include a reference to a saint. Successful Welsh premiership football team **The New Saints (TNS) [Y Seintiau Newydd] FC** owe their origins to a merger in 2004 between **Oswestry Town** and **Llansantffraid FC** (formerly **TNS – Total Network Solutions FC**), when a new name was cleverly coined that successfully retained the original **TNS** abbreviation, and also paid homage to the original nickname of the **Llansantffraid** club, derived from Saint Ffraid. Other football clubs in Wales that carry the nickname *Saints* include **Llansantffraid Village FC**, formed in 2007, **Merthyr Saints FC** (St. Tudful), **Presteigne Saint Andrews FC** (derived from the name of the parish church of St. Andreas), **St. Asaph City FC**, **St. Clears FC**, **St. Dogmael's FC**, **St. Florence FC** and Swansea Senior League side **St. Joseph's FC**. **Cardiff Civil Service FC** who once graced the Welsh League were also known as the *Saints*, a nickname derived from **St. Clair's FC**, the original name of the club. Rugby clubs that are known by the name *Saints* include **St. David's RFC** and **Senghennydd RFC** (attributable to a popular misinterpretation of the place-name as Saint Cenydd). **TATA Steel RFC** (formerly **Corus RFC**), of Port Talbot, are also known as the *Saints*, a name attributable to their merger with **St. Joseph's Old Boys RFC** which was undertaken to strengthen their player base. **Lampeter Town RFC**'s second XV are also known as the *Saints*.

Saracens / Sarries: The name is derived from Saladin's nomadic desert warriors of the twelfth century who fought against the Crusaders. **Newport Saracens RFC** at its outset in 1912 had no permanent base and as such were essentially 'nomadic'. Consequently they named themselves *Saracens*, influenced without doubt by **Saracens RFC**, founded some 40 years earlier. Both clubs are affectionately known as the *Sarries*. **Cardiff Saracens RFC** is a Welsh Districts rugby team.

Scarlet Bulldogs: Ferndale RFC. The club was founded in 1882 and enjoyed considerable success especially during the period immediately before the Great War. In 1910 and 1912 the famous *Scarlet Bulldogs* won two major trophies. The club folded in 1921 owing to the difficult economic climate, and was not reformed until 1989.

Scarlets / Scarlet Runners: Llanelli RFC / Llanelli Scarlets RFC / Scarlets RFC. Founded in 1872, **Llanelli RFC**, one of the most iconic rugby clubs in the world, and nicknamed the *Scarlets*, did not actually play in their famous colours until Easter Monday 1884 when the team took the field for the first time in scarlet jerseys – complete with scarlet gold braided caps against a team called County Dublin drawn from the full Irish team who had played Wales on the previous Saturday and who chose to play an additional fixture on their way home. *The Llanelly & County Guardian*, 17 April 1884, reported on the match in detail which ended in an honourable draw, and commented very favourably on the team's 'bright appearance' in their new jerseys. Inititially the team was dubbed the *Scarlet Runners* by the local press, before *Runners* was later dropped. The nickname *Scarlets* became very well established during the twentieth century, and with the advent of regional rugby in 2003 continuity was maintained with the adoption of the team name **Llanelli Scarlets RFC.** This was later simplified to **Scarlets RFC** in 2008 as it was deemed to be more inclusive and representative of a large region which also incorporated north and mid-Wales. When the club moved to their new ground in the Pemberton district of Llanelli in November 2008 the stadium was appropriately named *Parc-y-Scarlets*. **Pembroke RFC**, also nicknamed the *Pembrokeshire Scarlets*, traditionally play in scarlet coloured shirts with white shorts and scarlet socks. **Tylorstown RFC** were once known as the *Scarlets* in the period prior to 1907 when they played on Cae Tŷ Gwyn. They later changed their playing field and colours and became well-known as the *Tigers*. The earliest use of the nickname I have seen is for the **Blaenavon Scarlet Runners RFC**, recorded in 1880–81.

Scorpions: South Wales Scorpions RLFC. The *Scorpions* are a professional rugby team based at the Gnoll, Neath, home of **Neath RFC**. The club adopted the name **South Wales Scorpions RLFC** on 22 December 2009 following a competition won by Mr James Bowes of Cardiff. Scorpions are predatory animals easily recognisable by their impressive claws.

SCOWS: TATA Steel FC and **TATA Steel RFC.** The former works teams of the Port Talbot steel plant, are still occasionally known as the

SCOWS, an acronym of the name Steel Company of Wales, formed in 1947, which was absorbed into British Steel following the nationalisation of the industry in 1967. The teams subsequently became known as **British Steel FC / RFC**, subsequently **Corus Steel FC / RFC** until the company was again taken over by TATA Steel Europe Ltd. in 2010 resulting in a further name change.

Scrumpies: Pyle RFC. The club, formed during the inter-war period, originally had *Ye Olde Wine House* (generally known as 'The Tap') as its headquarters. The public house's best-selling brew was rough cider (or scrumpy), which became a favourite tipple with the players; it was also considerably cheaper than beer. As a consequence, the nickname *Scrumpies* became attached to **Pyle RFC**, and when a club badge was later commissioned it incorporated a cider apple.

Seagulls: Famously the nickname of **Brighton & Hove Albion FC**, there are also some examples of its adoption in Wales. **Colwyn Bay FC, Fishguard & Goodwick RFC, Hundleton FC** and **Sully FC** (who merged with **Inter Cardiff FC** to form **UWIC Inter Cardiff FC**) are commonly known as the *Seagulls*, and all four teams carry the seabird on their club crests. The adoption of the seagull as the emblem of **Hundleton FC** of the Pembrokeshire Football League has a particularly interesting history. It is based on a work of fiction, entitled *Seagull Billy*, the story of a tame seagull, first published in 1929, and written by Winifred M. Hitchings, where she relates the childhood memories of her disabled brother Horace Hitchings of Hundleton, at a time when their father John Hitchings was headmaster of Orielton School from 1889 to 1898.

Seahawks: Fishguard RFC's second XV are known as the *Seahawks*. The *Seahawk* is another name for the Osprey, or other predatory seabirds such as the Autumn passage Arctic Skua and Great Skua sometimes seen off the Pembrokeshire coastline.

Seahorses: Colwyn Bay RFC. The seahorse, a mythical marine creature, is prominent on the club's emblem. The nickname is most probably a metaphor for seasideness.

Seasiders: In common with many football teams located in coastal resorts, notably **Blackpool FC**, a number of Welsh teams share this nickname with the club from Lancashire. These include **Aberaeron FC, Afan Lido FC, Aberystwyth Town FC** (with its mascot *Sami Seagull*), **Barmouth & Dyffryn United FC, Llansteffan FC, Llantwit Major FC, New Quay FC, Porth-cawl FC** and **Prestatyn Town FC**. Rugby clubs **Mumbles RFC, Penarth RFC** and **Tenby United RFC,** based in major holiday towns, are also known as the *Seasiders*. **Porth-cawl RFC**, now usually referred to as the *Seaweeds*, were once known as the *Seasiders*. *See also:* **Pride of the Seaside**

Seaweeds: Porth-cawl RFC. Although known as the *Seaweeds*, the club emblem actually shows a seagull. In earlier times **Porth-cawl RFC** were known as the *Seagulls*.

Seintiau *see:* **Saints**

Sêr *see:* **Stars**

Seven: Seven Sisters FC / Seven Sisters RFC. *Seven* is often used as an abbreviated version of the place-name as, for example, in the title of the rugby club's centenary booklet, *The magnificent Seven*, written by Dr. Hywel Francis in 1997. The village takes its name from the Seven Sisters colliery, said to commemorate the seven sisters of Evan Evans Bevan, son of Evan Evans of Neath and partner with David Bevan in various colliery undertakings.

Sharks: The suffix adopted by the **West Wales Sharks RLFC** and **Dinefwr Sharks RLFC**, two short-lived amateur rugby league teams. The name *Sharks* in rugby circles is most famously associated with South Africa's Super 12 union team **KwaZulu Natal Sharks RFC** based at Durban. It has also been adopted by **Ynysowen Sharks RFC**.

Sheep: A nickname once applied to **UWIC Inter Cardiff FC,** and attributable to Wales' association with sheep farming. **Defaid Du FC** [Black Sheep] were until very recently a Montgomeryshire League side based at Llandrinio, Powys. Their imaginative name was apparently based on the fact that many of their players had less than spotless criminal records!

Shoppies / Shoppoes: A nickname applied to teams who played on half-day closing. Examples include **Neath Allied Traders RFC** ('The Shoppoes') and **Treherbert Shoppies RFC** who both played prior to the Second World War. *See also:* **Wednesday/s; Thursdays**

Silkmen: Flint Town United FC. A nickname attributable to the importance of the artificial silk industry in the town, started by a subsidiary of a German company, the British Glanzstoff Manufacturing Company, in 1907. During the Great War the factory closed down but was taken over by Courtaulds in 1917, which built two new large plants at nearby Greenfield. At its peak these factories were employing over 3,000 workers in the manufacture of the synthetic fibre viscose rayon. The factories were all decommissioned by the 1980s. *The Silkworm* was the published fanzine of supporters of the *Silkmen*. The original *Silkmen* were **Macclesfield Town FC**, as the Cheshire town was at one time the world's largest producer of finished silk, boasting over 70 mills as early as 1832.

Silverbacks: The second XV of **New Tredegar RFC** are known as the *Silverbacks*. The Rwanda national rugby team are also known as the *Silverbacks*, named after the country's signature mountain gorillas.

Skull & Crossbones: Rhyl Skull & Crossbones FC. A very early team formed in the 1870s in Rhyl which competed in the Welsh Cup. The players wore the pirate motif on their black shirts to strike fear into their opponents. The symbol became popular with several sporting organisations, especially in towns with a strong maritime tradition. As noted under **Blue & Blacks**, it was used at one time by **Cardiff RFC**.

Skullcrackers: Brynaman RFC. A rather unflattering nickname coined by fierce local rivals **Cwmllynfell RFC** for their neighbours and prevalent during the early years of the twentieth century. **Diamond Skullcrackers RFC** are also recorded in 1898 as an early rugby team in Carmarthen town.

Sky Blues: Cambrian & Clydach FC of the Welsh League share their nickname with **Coventry City FC** reflecting the playing colours of both teams. A works team based at Newtown, **GKN [Guest, Keen & Nettlefolds] Sports FC**, who manufactured transmission systems for the car industry, fielded a team in the Montgomeryshire Football League for 15 years from 1965 until the closure of the factory in the early 1980s and were also known as the *Sky Blues*. *See also:* **Blues**

Smitw: Ynysmeudwy Athletic FC. The local pronunciation of the village name, also applied as a nickname to the football team, and based on the rich dialect of the Swansea Valley. Sadly, it appears to have been supplanted by the rather unimaginative *Ynys* in recent press reports.

Snakes: Aberdare RFC. The team is known by the nickname *Snakes*, which is also still commonly used as a name for the town's people, especially by the neighbouring people of Merthyr. Its origins are unclear, and several theories have been advanced. Outsiders have tried to propagate the version which claimed that it is connected with the willingness of some Aberdare miners to break the 1912 strike and 'snake' their way back to work. Another kinder version claims that Aberdare workers walked over the mountain to Merthyr to work in the iron furnaces, and as they carried candles they would be visible for many miles 'snaking' their way down the mountain. Aberdare people would prefer to support the well-documented version that the Cynon Valley, in pre-industrial times, was infested with adders, a fact noted by the Revd Jabez Edmund Jenkins (1840–1903) in his *Vaynor, its history and guide*, published in 1879. Jenkin Howell writing in 1903 failed to offer an explanation for the name.

Snowdonians: Llanberis FC. An early local press nickname derived from the fact that the village is situated at the foot of Mount Snowdon.

Sosban: Scarlets RFC / Llanelli RFC: Llanelli, always known as *tref y sosban* [saucepan town] on account of its tin plating industry which was largely associated with the mass production of cheap saucepans and kitchen utensils for the British and overseas markets. The town's links with the industry led to the adoption of the humorous Welsh folk song,

Sosban Fach, as the unofficial anthem of the local rugby supporters. The *Sosban* has featured prominently in many of the club's activities and has manifested itself in many ways. The chorus has also been adapted into English so as to remind the opposition of the club's most historic achievements:

> "Who beat the All Blacks or Who beat the Walla –
> Wallabies – But good old Sosban Fach."

Not only is the club often referred to by the nickname *Sosban*, the club has ensured that the connection is given every possible exposure as an effective marketing tool. A miniature saucepan serves as the supporter's club badge, and two flat shaped red and white saucepans were placed on top of the rugby posts at Stradey Park, a practice that has continued at their new home, Parc-y-Scarlets. The east stand at Parc-y-Scarlets also has *SOSBAN* etched in white seating as a stand-out feature. *Sosban* is also the name of a recently opened award-winning restaurant in Llanelli.

Spa / Spamen: Llandrindod Wells FC. Attributable to the significance of the healing waters associated with the town which led to a significant boom during the Victorian and Edwardian eras.

Spinners: The nickname of the **British Nylon Spinners RFC**, the works team of the prestigious factory which was established at Pontypool in 1948, and which operated until its closure in 1988. The factory once boasted the largest floorspace in Europe and was a major employer in the western valleys of Monmouthshire.

Sports: Bridgend Sports RFC, Evans & Williams Sports FC, Fishguard Sports FC, Saundersfoot Sports FC and **Sully Sports RFC.** An abbreviation of the team's name and generally used when a range of sports is played by the club in question.

Squirrels: Rhiwbina RFC. The club was established in 1962, following a public meeting held at the *Butchers' Arms*. Apparently the *Squirrels* nickname and logo was chosen for the club after noticing that one of the beer pumps in the public house had a squirrel emblem on its handle. The red squirrel was originally the logo of Holt's Brewery in Aston, Birmingham. It was eventually taken over by Ansells Brewery and used to identify their own beers.

Stags: Blaengarw RFC. The Ogmore Vale club is known as the *Stags,* and the animal has also been incorporated into the club's emblem.

STAR: An acronym rather than a nickname for **STAR** (St. Mellon's, Trowbridge & Rumney) **RFC**, a community club who play at the Cath Cobb Fields, St. Mellon's on the eastern outskirts of Cardiff.

Starch: Gowerton RFC: People from Gowerton are often referred to as the *Starch*, and the name has also been associated with the rugby team. It apparently derives from the period when the area processed steel destined for export to all parts of the globe. The steel owners and white collar workers all tended to reside in the posher Gowerton area, giving rise to the nickname *Starch*, indicating snobby-ness. The name lives on in a *Facebook* page, '*The Gowerton Starch*'.

Stars (Sêr): A common suffix for both football and rugby teams. **Cwm-carn Stars RFC**, formed in 1888 are the forerunners of the present **Cwm-carn United RFC. Crynant RFC** are known as the *Stars*, and the emblem of the club includes a picture of a white horse and a star that represents the original clubhouse, the *Star Hotel*. The nickname *Stars* was used in the title of David Alexander's club history published in 1991 – *Stars on a Saturday*. The author tells an amusing story which relates to the surreptitious activities of the junior team sometime after the Great War. During this period a Mr Walbrook ran a temporary cinema in the village housed in a tent. As most of the films he showed were American, a stars and stripes flag was flown above the marquee. The local youngsters grasped an opportunity to make use of the flag in a practical way! Quietly one evening they removed the flag and cut out the white stars which were then sewn on their red shirts! Among many other teams using the suffix *Stars* are: **Aberavon Green Stars RFC, Blackwood Stars RFC, Cwm-bach Royal Stars FC, Dewi Stars (Sêr Dewi) FC** (captain of the team in the 1920s was Jimmy Mann, son of Arthur Mann, a tailor who sewed the red stars on the team's white shirts), **New Dock Stars RFC, Port Talbot Blue Stars FC** and **Treowen Stars FC.**

Newtown White Stars FC, forerunners of **Newtown FC,** defeated **Wrexham FC** to win the Welsh Cup in 1879; the name has been revived by the club's present junior section. **Troedyrhiw Stars FC** were a major force in Welsh football during the early years of the twentieth century and **Cathan Stars FC**, from Garnswllt near Ammanford, captained by the father of Dai Davies, the international goalkeeper, played for almost forty years in the Carmarthenshire League until their demise in 1967. **Sêr Ceredigion Stars DFC** is a pan-disability football team formed in 2007 and based at Aberaeron and Aberystwyth who play on a monthly basis against similar teams from other parts of Wales. The **White Stars RFC** were an early rugby team established at Nant-y-moel playing during the 1885–86 season. **Grange Stars RFC** were an early Cardiff rugby team operating before the Great War.

Steelers: Neath Port Talbot Steelers RLFC. The name replicates many famous teams such as the American football team **Pittsburgh Steelers** and ice hockey team **Sheffield Steelers** who also play in steel-making towns. The team was formerly known as **Aberavon Fighting Irish RLFC.**

Steelmen (Dynion Dur): In common with many other steel making towns such as Corby and Motherwell, football teams based in Welsh steel making centres have also carried the nickname *Steelmen*. These include **Brymbo FC**, once a very successful team, formed initially in 1943 as a works team. The nickname *Steelmen* has continued in common use in spite of the closure of the works since 1990. **Port Talbot FC** of the Welsh Premiership also carry the same name, as do their neighbours **TATA Steel FC** and **Llanwern AFC** on the outskirts of Newport. In the rugby union code **Ebbw Vale RFC** provides another example. Reflecting its past significance as a centre of heavy industry, the nickname *Steelmen* is still in common usage in spite of final closure of the large Ebbw Vale steelworks in 2002. *Dynion Dur,* the Welsh equivalent of *Steelmen*, is also given prominence on the Club's website. **Ebbw Vale FC** were also known as the *Steelmen* until the adoption of the nickname *Cowboys.* The club folded in 1998.

Street: The nickname of **Bridgend Street FC**, Splott, Cardiff. **Bow**

Street FC is often referred to in the local press as *Street,* rather than by its more traditional nickname of *Magpies.*

Strikers: Newport Strikers LFC. The *Strikers* were a successful ladies' football team who competed in the South West Women's Football League in the 1990s.

Strollers: Ton Strollers FC. The name of one of the thirteen founder members of the South Wales League, presumably based at Ton Pentre in the Rhondda Valley.

Suburbs: Porth Tywyn Suburbs FC. The team played in the Welsh League from 1993 until 2004, and are based at Suburbs Park, Burry Port, near Llanelli. They currently play in the Carmarthenshire League. The team was formed as **Burry Port Garden Suburbs FC** in 1921 and named after one of several social housing projects prevalent at the time. Porth Tywyn is the Welsh name for Burry Port.

Super Daffs *see:* **Daffs**

Super Reds: Llanfairpwll FC. A nickname prevalent in the 1970s when the team, under the successful management of Owen (Now) Parry, played in all-red strip, influenced by the nickname and success of **Liverpool FC.** *See also:* **Reds**

Supertaffs: A nickname for **Cardiff City** FC prevalent as a chant among fans in the early 1970s. *See also:* **Taffs**

Swallows: Llandysul FC. The bird is also incorporated into the club's emblem. There is no obvious reason for the choice of name, but the proximity of the river Teifi to the club's playing field, and its abundant airborne insect life would provide a natural feeding ground for the swallow. The team also play in blue which is one of the swallow's prominent colours.

Swans (Elyrch): Familiarly the nickname of **Swansea City FC,** an abbreviated form of Swansea, giving rise to the club's symbol and white playing colours, and which was in use by the local press very soon after the club's foundation as **Swansea Town FC** in 1912. Recently, in Swansea Central Library, the discovery was made of a *Swans' War Song,* dated 1913, the words of which were set to the tune of *Chocolate Major,* a music hall favourite, providing further evidence that the nickname was in use from the very early days of the club. The chorus ran as follows:

"We are the Swans' supporters, we are the village boys
When our team is playing, hear us all hurrahing."

More recently the nickname has gained widespread publicity through the activities of *Cyril the Swan,* the club's once controversial mascot, but now much placated after his marriage to his wife Sybil, and especially well-behaved since Premiership football came to the city! *Elyrch* is a well-established Welsh equivalent and was used recently in Geraint Jenkins' centenary volume, *Yr Elyrch: dathlu'r 100* (2012). Rugby teams **Caldicot RFC** and their footballing neighbours **Caldicot Town FC** have also adopted the swan symbol as it was the family crest of the De Bohun family of Caldicot Castle. **Aber-carn RFC** also include a swan on their team crest in recognition of the importance of the *Swan Inn* as their first headquarters.

Swansea Jacks: *see* Jacks

Swansea Wellingtons: West End FC.
A nickname applied to the Mayhill, Swansea Welsh League club founded at the *Wellington* public house, Garden Street, Swansea in 1964.

Swanselona: Swansea City FC.
A nickname which was applied to **Swansea City FC** during their first season in the Premiership, 2011–12 as they were rather flatteringly compared to **FC Barcelona** for their passing style of football.

Swifts:
Teams known by this nickname include the **Holyhead Swifts FC** who competed in the North Wales Coast League in the early years of the twentieth century, **Llandudno Swifts FC**, who competed in the Welsh League (North) in the 1970s, **Monkton Swifts FC** of the Pembrokeshire League and **St. Harmon & District FC** of Radnorshire all

of which include the swift motif on their club crests. The **Tenby Swifts RFC** merged with **Tenby Harlequins RFC** in 1901 to form **Tenby United RFC**. The bird, a member of the *Apodidae* family, is associated with speed and gracefulness.

Taffies *see:* **Thames Taffies**

Taffs: Taff's Well FC. Probably a shortened version of the place-name. *Taff* is, however, a nickname associated with Welsh persons, taking its name from the river Taf(f) which flows through the village. *See also:* **Supertaffs; Thames Taffies**

Tatters *see:* **Rags / Rags & Tatters**

Teifisiders: A nickname applied to many teams located in the towns and villages of the Teifi Valley.

Teigrod *see:* **Tigers**

Teirw Duon: Clwb Rygbi Tregaron RFC, established in 1975, were known as *Y Teirw Duon* [Black Bulls], or *Crysau Duon* during their formative years. The name reflected their playing colours of black shirts, and alliterated with the name of the town. However, the club's badge, designed by local artist and schoolteacher Ogwyn Davies, depicts a snipe, a bird commonly found on the renowned nature reserve at neighbouring Cors Caron (Tregaron Bog).

Teirw Nant Conwy: Clwb Rygbi Nant Conwy RFC. The club based at Trefriw in the Vale of Conwy are nicknamed *Teirw Nant Conwy* (Nant Conwy Bulls). The club badge consists of the head of a black bull over the club's name. *See also:* **Bulls**

Terriers: Wattstown RFC's second XV are known as the *Terriers*. The name *Terriers* was coined as "a bit of clubhouse banter" because the club's long-serving first team captain is named Michael Tinson – hence *Tinson's Terriers*. The name is popular as a suffix for rugby teams, especially in Yorkshire because of its association with the Yorkshire Terrier breed. It is also the official nickname of **Huddersfield Town FC**, a club located in the West Riding.

Thames Taffies: A rather derogatory nickname applied to **London Welsh RFC.**

Thin Red Line: Rhayader Town FC. Football was first played at Rhayader in 1889, and during their first decade they earned themselves the nickname *Thin Red Line*, which remains in common use. The name arose because of the rather original solution they devised to resolve the problem of when their colours clashed with that of the opposition. To distinguish themselves from their opponents they resorted to using red ribbons obtained from a local draper which were then worn diagonally on their existing shirts.

Thursdays: *Thursdays*, as with other teams that carry the suffix *Wednesday*, including the famous Yorkshiremen, **Sheffield Wednesday FC**, reflect teams originally formed to play on half-day closing days. In Wales these include **Aberdare Thursdays FC** and **Ammanford Thursdays FC**, who both played in the 1920s and 1930s, and the more well-known **Abergavenny Thursdays FC**, who are still in existence. In Abergavenny's case the opposition was provided by teams competing in the Hereford Thursday League. Also in the 1920s, in neighbouring Talgarth, a team called the **Talgarth Early Closers FC** competed in the Mid-Wales League. *See also:* **Shoppies / Shoppoes; Wednesday/s**

Tigers / Teigars / Teigrod: A common nickname, famously associated with **Hull City FC**, for teams who play in black and amber. **CPD Llanberis FC**, sometimes called *Y Teigars,* play in amber shirts and black shorts (possibly influenced by the horseracing colours of the Assheton Smith family who owned the local Dinorwig slate quarry) as do **Trallwm FC** of the Carmarthenshire League. **Menai Bridge Tigers FC (CPD Teigrod Porthaethwy)** play in striped amber and black shirts. Other teams nicknamed the *Tigers* include **Port Talbot Tigers FC**, established in 2003. **Cardigan Town FC** were also known as the *Tigers* during the post war-period. In rugby circles the name is most commonly associated with **Leicester Tigers RFC**, a name, dating from

1885, which probably owes its origins to the presence of the Royal Leicestershire Regiment in India which earned them the nickname *Tigers*. However, in the case of Welsh rugby teams, such as **Taibach RFC** and **Tylorstown RFC** the nickname is attributable to the black and amber hoops of their club shirts. **Pen-y-banc RFC** are also known as the *Tigers* and **Cimla Tigers RFC** are a Welsh Districts rugby club. **Torfaen Tigers RLFC**, based at Pontypool, play in black with amber stripes on their shorts. **Mardy Tigers FC,** a club founded in 2003 and based in Abergavenny, provide a range of football opportunities for girls aged under 16 years. The club has recently formed a senior ladies team who play under the name of **PILCS LFC**.

'Tillery: Abertillery RFC. An abbreviation of the place-name.

Tinplaters: An early press nickname for **Llanelli RFC**, attributable to the town's famous tinplate industry. The name was also applied to **Aberaman FC** for the same reason.

Tirion: Bryntirion Athletic FC. The progressive Bridgend-based club are often referred to as *The Tirion*, an abbreviated form of the place-name.

Tish: St. Ishmael's FC. The Pembrokeshire League club is affectionately known as *Tish*. The nickname is derived from 'St. Ish...'.

Titans: Titans RLFC. Formerly **Newport Titans RLFC,** the club was formed in 2004, evolving from **Rumney Rhinos RLFC.** In 2011 they abandoned the preface Newport when they re-located to Machen. A *Titan* was any one of a family of giants in Greek mythology and ruling the earth until overthrown by the Olympian gods.

Toffeemen: Formed in 1918 **Lovell's Athletic FC** were the works team of G. F. Lovell & Co., Ltd., confectionery manufacturers of Newport and makers of *Toffee Rex*, 'King of the Toffees', which gave rise to the nickname *Toffeemen*. They were a very successful football team that played in the Western, Southern and Welsh leagues, winning the Welsh Cup in 1948, and were crowned Welsh League champions on six occasions. They disbanded in 1969 with the closure of the firm. **Everton FC** are also known as the *Toffees*, and several theories have been advanced for its derivation, but it is likely that it was associated with Everton toffee which was made in that district of Liverpool.

Ton: Tongwynlais FC. An abbreviation of the place-name.

Tramps: The nickname of **Canton Wanderers RFC**, an early Cardiff & District rugby union team playing before the Great War. *Tramps* is presumably a variation of *Wanderers*. *See also:* **Trotters; Wanderers**

Traws: Familiarly an abbreviation for the village of Trawsfynydd in Gwynedd, and applied to **Trawsfynydd FC** who played in the Cambrian Coast Football League from 1947–48 until their demise in 1956–57. Originally formed as **Prysor Rovers FC** in 1946–47, they changed their name after only one season. The river Prysor now runs into Llyn Trawsfynydd, a man-made lake originally created for hydro-electric purposes, but later utilised for the supply of cooling water to the nuclear reactor built on the edge of the village in the 1960s. The nickname *Traws* has also, without any real foundation, been applied by the local press to Ceredigion team **Traws-goed FC**.

Troggs: Trinant RFC. A nickname applied to the people of Trinant in Caerphilly Borough and its rugby team. *Troggs* is a shortened form of *Trogolytes*, or cave dwellers! The origin is uncertain, but it is probably a play on the first two letters of the village's name, and is possibly influenced by the pop group Troggs who had several hits in the 1960s including *Wild Thing* and *Love is all around*.

Trotters: Buckley Town FC. Probably a variant on *Wanderers*, another of the club's nicknames inherited from the merger of **Buckley Rovers** and **Buckley Wanderers** in 1949. **Bolton Wanderers FC** are also known as the *Trotters*, although other less convincing explanations have been advanced for the nickname.

Tudno: Llandudno FC. A nickname which derives from Saint Tudno who gave his name to the town.

Turfs: Tregaron Turfs FC. The term *Turfs* was first coined for a team in Tregaron during the period after the Great War in 1919 when they played on land adjacent to Cors Caron (Tregaron Bog) where turf cutting for peat was a prevalent activity.

Turks: Trefechan FC. The powerful and feared **Trefechan FC** team that once played in the Aberystwyth & District Football League were known as the *Turks*, a name applied to inhabitants of this area of Aberystwyth. The nickname may simply be derived from the initial two letters of the village's name. However, other more interesting explanations have been advanced. A letter in the *Welsh Gazette,* published in 1900, recalls a Turkish ship that was wrecked south of Trefechan, and the people of the village apparently showed a lot of kindness to the victims, which in turn may have given rise to their nickname of *Turks*. Iwan Wmffre considers that a more likely explanation would be an emulation of *Turkey Shore* – a nickname prevalent as early as the eighteenth century for the inhabitants of the south bank of the river Thames in London, because they were considered to be as wild and uncouth as the people of Turkey! Areas known as *Turkey Shore* are also found adjacent to the docks at Caernarfon and Holyhead. People from Llanelli are also nicknamed *Turks*, especially by their *Jack* neighbours in Swansea. The origin of this name is also uncertain, but one theory that has been advanced is that many Turkish sailors once called at the port of Llanelli during their voyages.

'Twrch: Cwm-twrch RFC. The village takes its name from the river *Twrch* [wild boar], and the boar's head has been the club's emblem since its inception. The story features in the Arthurian legend *Culwch ac Olwen* as told in the *Mabinogion*. The legend relates to one of many tasks set by the giant Ysbadden for Culwch to undertake successfully before he would be allowed to marry his daughter Olwen. One task was to rid the Brecon Beacons of the pack of wild boars that were terrorising the people, and Culwch enlisted the support of King Arthur to achieve this. Arthur chased the *Twrth Trwyth* from Dyfed eastward towards Powys, and on the Black Mountain range, he picked up a large stone (*carreg fryn fras*) and cast it towards the wild animals, killing the leader of the pack on the edge of a valley near Craig-y-frân gorge. The large boar's body rolled down the valley and into the river which is now the river Twrch. The *Twrch* also features on the badge of **Ammanford FC**, and recently a metal boar sculpture with piglets has been commisioned and erected on an approach road to the town. *See also:* **Bears; Tyrch's; Wild Boars**

'Tws: Bettws RFC. An abbreviated form of the place-name.

Tybïe: Llandybïe RFC. The name derives from the place-name Llandybïe, [Church of Tybïau], thought to be one of the many daughters of the legendary Brychan Brycheiniog.

Tyrch's: Pen-tyrch RFC. *Tyrch* is the plural form of *twrch*, meaning boar. *See also:* **Twrch**

Unedig *see:* **United**

Unicorns: Founded in 1934, **Nelson RFC,** has the fabled creature, a white unicorn, on a black background as its emblem, and the nickname *Unicorns* is now well-established. **Cwmmaman Institute FC** and **Landore Colts Rangers FC** also feature the unicorn on their club crests.

United (Unedig): A popular suffix for football teams, usually indicating a merger of two or more teams. It is believed that **Sheffield United FC** were the first football team to adopt it in 1889, and others such as **Newcastle United FC** followed in 1892. Many Welsh teams have carried the suffix, notably **Ammanford United FC**, **Borough United FC, Goytre United, Milford United FC** and **West End United FC. West End United FC**, a Llanelli-based Carmarthenshire League team formed in 1988, adopted the suffix *United* so as to avoid confusion with neighbours **West End FC**, the Welsh League team based in the Mayhill district of Swansea. The Llanelli team was named **West End United FC** by its founder Ray Jones as they met in the the *Princess' Head* public house located in an area of the town known as the West End. The suffix *United* has also been applied to rugby union teams such as **Amman United RFC, Pontypool United RFC** and **Tenby United RFC.** The Welsh equivalent *Unedig* is occasionally used to describe **Manchester United FC (Manceinion Unedig)**, but even the Welsh language comedy series *C'mon Midffild* opted for an English suffix for the fictitious **Bryn-coch United**. **Unedig Pen-y-bryn FC** were recently established in the Wrexham area.

Uplands: Swansea Uplands RFC. The team was so named after it was founded at the *Uplands Hotel,* Swansea in 1919.

Usksiders: An early nickname for **Newport RFC** recorded in the *Western Mail,* 25 January 1902.

Vale (Y Fêl): CPD Nantlle Vale FC. Known as the *Vale,* or locally in this predominantly Welsh-speaking area as *Y Fêl.* The team was a real force in the 1950s and boasted a fearsome half-back line which featured the late Orig Williams (1931–2009), a ruthless tackler who later became a successful professional wrestler.

Valley Commandos: The name suggested by Owen Smith MP and his supporters who revived the campaign in January 2012 for a fifth Welsh regional rugby side centred on **Bridgend RFC**, **Pontypridd RFC** and the Valleys. The name is also used to denote the present **Pontypridd RFC** team.

Venga Boys: Venture Community FC (CPD Y Fentur). The nickname has been recorded for this community club who play in the Welsh League (Wrexham Area). The name is probably derived from the Dutch pop group of the same name as it chimes with Venture.

Vets: An abbreviation of *Veterans,* and commonly used especially for middle-aged rugby teams.

Vics / Victoria: Knighton Victoria FC. The Powys team founded in 2010, are nicknamed the *Vics.* Victoria is often abbreviated to *Vic* in theatre and public house names.

Vikings: Hakin United FC. Hakin is located on the northern shore of Milford Haven, where the invading Vikings occasionally wintered, and created some permanent settlements. Around 854 AD Viking Chieftain

Hubba sheltered in the Haven with as many as 23 ships and gave his name to the parish of Hubberston which includes the village of Hakin. The nickname *Vikings* pays homage to these early settlers.

Villa / Villans: Hawkesbury Villa FC and **Prendergast Villa FC.** Probably copied from **Aston Villa FC**, a name that derives from an eighteenth-century residence known as Aston Villa. Teams with the suffix *Villa* are usually nicknamed *Villans*.

Village / Villagers: Brynteg Village FC and **Garden Village FC** are predictably nicknamed the *Village*. **Dinas Powys RFC** and **Rhydyfelin RFC** are also known as the *Villagers*.

Wanderers (Crwydriaid): A common name and suffix initially associated with **The Wanderers FC**, one of the earliest teams in England who, after a nomadic existence, eventually settled at the Kennington Oval. The team was successful and won the first FA Cup competition in 1872, and retained the trophy for the two succeeding years. With the growth of the professional game the team declined and eventually folded, but its name was popular and was adopted by several teams including, most famously **Bolton Wanderers FC**, founded in 1874 as **Christ Church FC**. The name was changed to **Bolton Wanderers FC** in 1877 following a dispute between Thomas Ogden, original founder of the club, and the local vicar, the Revd John Farrall Wright. The name *Wanderers* was chosen as the club initially had a lot of difficulty finding a permanent ground to play on, having used three venues in its first four years of existence. (**Wolverhampton Wanderers FC** adopted the name two years later than Bolton after merging with a local cricket club). Its first adoption in Wales was by **Phoenix Wanderers FC** of Pontypool, who were one of the founder members of the South Wales League in 1890. The name also features as a nickname or suffix for several other Welsh football and rugby clubs including **Buckley Town FC** (formed from a merger of **Buckley Wanderers FC** and **Buckley Rovers FC** in 1949), **Caernarfon Wanderers FC**, **Newton Wanderers FC** and **Ynys-y-bŵl Wanderers FC**. In rugby circles **Glamorgan Wanderers RFC [Crwydriaid Morgannwg]** (also known as the *Wands*), once one of the leading clubs in Wales, carry the name. Founded originally in 1893 as the **Old Monktonians RFC** by former pupils of Monkton House School, the name **Glamorgan Wanderers RFC** was adopted in 1913. They certainly lived up to their name and played on at least seven different home grounds until they eventually settled at the Memorial Ground, Ely, Cardiff in 1952. **Llanelli Wanderers RFC** also carry the suffix.

Warriors (Rhyfelwyr): The **Celtic Warriors RFC (Rhyfelwyr Celtaidd)** was the short-lived fifth Welsh regional rugby team, centred on **Bridgend RFC** and **Pontpridd RFC** which was disbanded after only one troublesome season. **Cleddau Warriors DFC** are a well-established disability football team based in Haverfordwest, and they have now been joined by another Pembrokeshire team named **Preseli Warriors DFC,** who operate from Fishguard.

Wasps (Picwn): A nickname traditionally accorded to teams who play in black and yellow striped or hooped shirts. The English rugby premiership team **London Wasps RFC** are probably the most famous club to don these colours. (They are often referred to as *Picwn,* the Welsh equivalent, in local television and radio commentaries). **Llangwm RFC**, the Pembrokeshire *Wasps*, founded in 1885, also play in the same colours and include a wasp on their club emblem. **Cornelly Wasps RFC** operated during the period following the Great War. **Dolgellau Athletic Amateur FC,** formed much later in 1971, are also known as the *Wasps*, and play in yellow and black striped shirts, and include the insect on their club emblem. **Clydach Wasps FC** from the Gwent League play in yellow shirts and black shorts.

Waterfallmen: Llanrhaeadr FC: The village of Llanrhaeadr-ym-Mochnant takes its name 'church of the waterfall' from the impressive *Pistyll Rhaeadr* located some four miles from the village. The waterfall, the single highest in the United Kingdom at 240 feet, is a major tourist attraction, and provides an apt nickname for the local football team.

Waterwheelers: Ton-du RFC. The club badge consists of a shield housing three Celtic crosses and a waterwheel symbolising the mill that once stood on the river Ogwr and associated with the woollen trade.

Pandy Park, the home of **Ton-du RFC**, takes its name from *pandy*, the Welsh for fulling mill.

Waun: Waunarlwydd RFC. The name is an abbreviation of the first element *(g)waun*, meaning moor.

Wddyn Boys: Llanwddyn FC. Former members of the Mont-gomeryshire Football League **Llanwddyn FC**, founded in 1948, were also known as the *Lake, Lakesiders*, or *Lord of the Lake*. The club played their home matches at Abertrinant, close to the Lake Vyrnwy dam at Llanwddyn, built in 1881–88 to supply water to Liverpool.

Wednesday/s: Teams originally established to play on half-day clos-ing such as **Brecon Wednesday FC, Builth Wednesdays FC** and **Llay Wednesday FC**, and more famously **Sheffield Wednesday FC**. *See also*: **Shoppies / Shoppoes; Thursdays**

Welfare: A once common suffix attached to teams connected with facil-ities provided by the Miners' Welfare movement from 1920 to 1951, notably playing fields. Examples include **Gwynfi Welfare FC** and **Glyn-neath Welfare FC**. As the importance of the mining industry declined, many teams abandoned the suffix *Welfare*. For example, **Glyn-neath Welfare FC** became **Glyn-neath Town FC** in 1973.

Wellingtons *see:* **Swansea Wellingtons**

Wellmen: Holywell Town FC. The nickname is a shortened version of the place-name. derived from the legend of Gwenfrewi which gave its name to the village. It describes her as being beheaded in the seventh cen-tury by a rejected suitor, her head rolling down a hill towards Beuno's Chapel, where a spring rose from the ground where the head came to rest. Her uncle Beuno later restored her to life, and a nunnery with Winifred as abbess was established around St. Winifred's Well, which became a place of pilgrimage. It is considered one of the Seven Wonders of Wales. **Taff's Well FC** shares the same nickname – the village taking its name from a medicinal well located in the village which stands on the river Taf. Both **Holywell Town FC** and **Taff's Well RFC** have incorporated a well on their club emblems.

Welsh All Blacks *see*: **All Blacks**

Welsh Wizards *see*: **Wizards**

Westenders: A nickname which has been recorded for **Connah's Quay Nomads FC**, a club formed in 1946. However, the name probably relates to an earlier team, **Connah's Quay & Shotton FC**, formed in 1920, which rented a playing field from the Northgate Brewery, at the rear of the *Halfway House* hotel. The team become members of the Welsh National League (North), as a fully professional outfit in 1922, but had folded by 1927. They acquired the nickname *Westenders* because the area around the *Halfway House* is located towards the west end of the town. **Connah's Quay Nomads FC** were founded in 1946, but actually played at the Halfway ground until 1997, inheriting the former nickname. Having moved to the Deeside Stadium, the name *Westenders* has now largely fallen into disuse, although the stadium is actually located on the same side of the town.

Western: Treharris Western FC. Treharris Athletic FC is thought to be the oldest football club in South Wales, and was founded in 1889. It was accepted into the Western League in 1906, winning the championship in 1910. The club later opted to join the Welsh League where it still plays. In 2010 it merged with **Western Hotel FC**, a Merthyr Football League team, sponsored by the *Great Western Hotel* in Treharris, and later adopted the name **Treharris Athletic Western**, an appropriate and relevant suffix in view of the club's early history.

White Stars: The **White Stars** were an early rugby team established at Nant-y-moel playing during the 1885–86 season. The name has been revived by a Sunday League football team known as **Nant-y-moel White Stars FC**. *See also:* **Stars**

Whites *see:* **All Whites; Black & Whites; Blue & Whites; Cherry & Whites; Green & Whites; Lilywhites; Red & Whites**

Wild Boars: West Wales Wild Boars RLFC. Founded in 2009, the *Wild Boars* were a short-lived amateur rugby league team based at St. Clears, Carmarthenshire. The name was probably chosen because of the boar's legendary associations with the area. *See also:* **'Twrch; 'Tyrch**

Wildcats: Tydfil Wildcats RLFC are an amateur rugby league club based at Dowlais, Merthyr Tudful.

Wingmakers: Airbus Broughton UK FC. The Welsh premiership football team which has its origins as a works-based team at the British aerospace factory in Broughton, Flintshire was once generally known as the *Planemakers*. As the factory now specialises in the production of aeroplane wings the team is today known by its more modern nickname of *Wingmakers*, a name which also appears on its club emblem.

Witches: Cwm-gwrach RFC. The club's emblem, a witch in full flight on her broomstick, reflects the name of the village 'Valley of the Witch', and has given rise to the nickname *Witches*.

Wizards: Aberavon RFC. Small red toy wizards adorn the tops of the rugby posts at their ground, and the figure of a wizard has appeared on the players' kit and the club's emblem since the mid-1970s. One theory on the origin of the nickname is based on the fact that many workers who came to Port Talbot in the nineteenth century were from the Carmarthen area, strongly associated with the legendary wizard Merlin. Many of these workers lived in one street named 'Carmarthen Row', close to where **Aberavon RFC**'s Talbot Athletic ground was built. However, the more generally accepted view is that the nickname was coined by *South Wales Evening Post* reporter Bill Taylor during the 1920s, when he dubbed the highly successful Aberavon team of that era *"The Wizards of the West"*. It may, however, owe its origins to a popular musical performed in south Wales theatres in the late nineteenth century entitled *The Great Wizard of the West*. **Merlin's Bridge FC** are also known as the *Wizards*, owing to the legendary association with the wizard Merlin. This has little credence as the original name of the village: situated near Haverfordwest in Pembrokeshire was 'Mawdlyn's Bridge' – the bridge (near the chapel) of Magdalen.

Wolves: Cefn Coed FC. Not strictly a nickname, but the wolf is used as the club's emblem. Its junior team is known as the *Wolf Cubs*. There is no onomastic evidence in the area to provide a link with the presence of *y blaidd* (wolf) in the area at one time, but the elements *cefn* + *coed* (wooded ridge) in Cefncoedycymer may provide a clue to its adoption.

Wyesiders: A nickname applied to teams who play in towns and villages through which this long river flows. Examples include **Builth Wells FC** and **Newbridge-on-Wye FC**.

Yellow Boys: Penmaen-mawr Phoenix FC. The nickname reflects the shirt colour of the team.

Yellow Canaries *see:* **Canaries**

Young Dragons: A nickname applied to the Wales under 21 national football team and its equivalent under 20 rugby union team.

Young Guns: Caerau (Ely) FC. Possibly derived from the popular Western film released in 1988 detailing the adventures of William H. Bonney (1859–81), better known as the outlaw *Billy the Kid.*

Zebras: A nickname, like *Magpies,* for teams that play in black & white. Teams include **Treorchy RFC** who play in black and white hooped shirts and have a zebra's head as their chosen emblem. Founded in 1886, they originally played in royal blue, and changed to their present colours in 1889. **Roath RFC**, nicknamed the *Zebras*, were an early pre-Great War Cardiff & District rugby team, who presumably also played in black and white. **Cefn Druids FC**, who play in black and white stripes, have also been referred to as the *Zebras*.

INDEX TO CLUB NAMES

Bradford Bulls RLFC (Bulls)

Brake Liners FC (Brake Liners)

Brecon Corinthians FC (Corries)

Brecon Wednesday FC (Wednesday/s)

Brickfield Rangers FC (Rangers)

Bridgend Athletic RFC (Athletic)

Bridgend Blue Bulls RLFC (Blue Bulls)

Bridgend Blue Dragons RLFC (Blue Dragons)

Bridgend Ravens RFC (Ravens) *see also:* All Blacks, Brewery Boys, Valley Commandos, Warriors

Bridgend Sports RFC (Sports)

Bridgend Street FC (Mission, Street)

Bridgend Town FC (Brewery Boys, Bridge) *see also:* Blue Dragons

Brighton & Hove Albion FC (Seagulls)

Brisbane Broncos RLFC (Broncos)

Bristol City FC (Robins)

Bristol Rovers FC (Rovers)

British & Irish Lions (Lions)

British Nylon Spinners RFC (Spinners)

British Steel FC (SCOWS)

British Steel RFC (SCOWS)

Briton Ferry Llansawel FC (Ferry)

Brithdir Bluebirds FC (Bluebirds)

Bro Ffestiniog CR / RFC (Quarrymen)

Brymbo FC (Steelmen)

Brynaman RFC (Greens, Skullcrackers)

Bryn-coch RFC (Eagles)

Bryn-coch United FC (United)

Bryn-crug FC *see:* Tywyn / Bryn-crug FC

Bryngwran Bulls FC (Bulls)

Brynithel RFC (Mighty Bryn, Owls)

Bryn-mawr RFC (City of the Hills Boys, Men of the Mawr)

Brynteg Village FC (Village / Villagers)

Bryntirion Athletic FC (Tirion)

Buckley Rovers FC *see:* Wanderers

Buckley Town FC (Bucks, Claymen, Trotters) *see also:* Wanderers

Buckley Wanderers FC (Trotters, Wanderers)

Builth Wednesdays FC (Wednesday/s)

Builth Wells FC (Black Ambers, Bulls, Wyesiders)

Builth Wells RFC (Bulls)

Burnley FC (Clarets)

Burry Port RFC (Blacks)

Burry Port Garden Suburbs FC (Suburbs)

Burton Albion FC (Brewers)

Buttrills Rovers FC *see:* Imps

Bwlch Rangers FC (Rangers)

Cadoxton Imps FC (Imps)

Caerau (Ely) FC (Young Guns)

Caerau All Whites FC (All Whites)

Caerau Athletic FC (Riverboaters)

Caereinion Old Boys Rugby Association RFC (COBRAS)

Caerffili see: Caerphilly

Caerleon FC (Romans)

Caerleon RFC (Helmets)

Caernarfon Athletic FC *see:* Canaries

Caernarfon CR / RFC (Cofis, Gogs)

Caernarfon (Carnarvon) Ironopolis FC ('Nops) *see also:* Canaries

Caernarfon Town FC (Canaries) *see also:* Cofis

Caernarfon Wanderers FC (Wanderers)

Caerphilly AFC (Jackdaws)

Caerphilly Castle LFC (Castle)

Caerphilly Druids FC (Druids)

Caerphilly RFC (Castlemen, Castletown Men, Cheesemen, Green & Whites, Harriers, Jackdaws,

Chepstow RFC (Black & Whites)

Chicago Bears (Bears)

Chirk AAA FC (Colliers)

Christ Church FC (Wanderers)

Churchstoke FC (Clarets)

CIACS RFC (CIACS)

Cilfynydd RFC (Cil)

Cimla Tigers RFC (Tigers)

Cleddau Warriors DFC (Warriors)

Clydach Wasps FC (Wasps)

Cogan Coronation FC (Coronation) *see also:* Ravens

Colwyn Bay FC (Seagulls)

Colwyn Bay RFC (Seahorses)

Connah's Quay & Shotton FC (Westenders)

Connah's Quay Nomads FC (Deesiders, Nomads, Westenders)

Conwy Borough FC (Castlemen, Musselmen) *see also:* Railwaymen

Corby Town FC (Steelmen)

Corinthians FC *see:* Corries

Cornelly Wasps RFC (Wasps)

Cornish Pirates RFC (Pirates)

Corus RFC (Saints, SCOWS)

Corwen FC (Reds)

Cosheston Cougars FC (Cougars)

Coventry City FC (Sky Blues)

CPC Bears RLFC (Bears)

Crayston Babes FC *see:* Dazzlers

Crewe Alexandra FC (Railwaymen) *see also:* Alex

Croesyceiliog FC (Croesy)

Croesyceiliog RFC (Cockerels, Croesy)

Crook Town FC (Black Ambers)

Cross Keys RFC (Keys)

Crusaders RLFC (Crusaders)

Crymych RFC (Men of Preseli / Preselimen)

Crynant RFC (Stars)

Cwm Albion Colts FC (Albion/s, Colts)

Cwm Albion FC (Albion/s)

Cwmamman Institute FC (Unicorns)

Cwmavon RFC (Reds)

Cwm-bach Harriers FC (Harriers)

Cwm-bach Royal Stars FC (Royal Stars)

Cwmbrân Celtic FC (Celtic / Celts)

Cwmbrân RFC (Crows)

Cwmbrân Town FC (Crows)

Cwm-carn Stars RFC (Stars)

Cwm-carn United RFC *see also:* All Blacks, Stars

Cwm-gors RFC (Cherries)

Cwm-gwrach RFC (Witches)

Cwmllynfell RFC (Blues) *see also:* Skullcrackers

Cwmtillery Excelsiors FC (Excelsiors)

Cwmtillery FC *see:* Excelsiors

Cwm-twrch RFC ('Twrch)

Cymmer RFC (Cape)

Cynon Valley Cougars RLFC (Cougars)

Dafen Welfare FC (Bluebirds, Rockets)

Dazzlers AFC (Dazzlers)

Dee Valley Dragons RLFC (Dragons)

Defaid Du FC (Bad Boys, Sheep)

Defiants FC (Defiants)

Deiniolen FC (Llanbabs)

Denbigh Town FC (Castlemen)

Deri Broncos RFC (Broncos)

Dewi Stars FC (Stars)

Diamond Skullcrackers RFC (Skullcrackers)

Dinas Powys FC *see:* Ravens

Dinas Powys RFC (Village / Villagers)

Dinefwr Sharks RLFC (Sharks)

Hafodyrynys RFC (Hafod)

Hakin United FC (Vikings)

Hamilton Academical FC
  (Academicals, Accies)

Harlech Town CPD/FC (Castlemen)

Haverfordwest County FC (Bluebirds)

Haverfordwest RFC (Blues)

Hawarden Rangers FC (Rangers)

Hawkesbury Villa FC (Villa / Villans)

Heart of Midlothian FC (Hearts)

Hendy RFC (Cherry & Whites)

Heol-y-Cyw RFC (Cockerels)

Herbrandston FC (Herbie)

Hibernian FC (Hibs)

Hirwaun RFC (Brocks)

Holt Nomads FC (Nomads)

Holyhead Hotspur FC (Harbourmen,
  Hotspur)

Holyhead RFC (Harbourmen)

Holyhead Swifts FC (Swifts)

Holyhead Town FC (Harbourmen)

Holywell Arcadians FC (Arcadians)

Holywell Town FC (Wellmen)

Huddersfield Town FC (Terriers)

Hull City FC (Tigers)

Hundleton FC (Seagulls)

Inter Cardiff FC *see:* Seagulls

Internazionale Milan FC *see:*
  International

Kenfig Hill FC (Lilywhites, Reds,
  Riversiders)

Kenfig Hill Harlequins RFC (Ganzies)

Kenfig Hill Juniors FC (Burglars)

Kenfig Hill RFC (All Whites,
  Cavaliers, Mules) *see also:* Ganzies

Kidwelly FC (Black Cats)

Kidwelly RFC (Black & Ambers)

Killay FC *see:* Clarets

King's Lynn FC (Linnets)

Kingsbridge Colts FC (Colts)

Knighton Town FC (Borderers,
  Radnor Robins)

Knighton Victoria FC (Vics / Victoria)

KwaZulu Natal Sharks RFC (Sharks)

Lampeter Town FC (Magpies)

Lampeter Town RFC (Maroons,
  Saints) *see also:* Fighting Parsons

Landore Colts Rangers FC (Colts) *see
  also:* Unicorns

Laugharne RFC (Cocklemen,
  Laugharnees)

Leeds Rhinos RLFC (Rhinos)

Leicester City FC (Foxes)

Leicester Tigers RFC (Tigers)

Leinster Rugby RFC (Boys in Blue)

Lex XI FC (Lawmen)

Leyton Orient FC (O's)

Lisvane-Heath Hornets FC (Hornets)

Liverpool FC *see:* Super Reds

Llanbabo CPD / FC (Llanbabs)

Llanberis Comrades FC (Comrades)

Llanberis CPD / FC (Berries, Black &
  Ambers, Darans, Locos,
  Snowdonians, Tigers)

Llanboidy FC (Foxes)

Llandaff North RFC (North)

Llandegfan Antelope FC (Antelopes)

Llandovery RFC (Drovers)

Llandrindod Wells FC (Spa / Spamen)

Llandudno FC (Tudno)

Llandudno Junction FC (Railwaymen)

Llandudno RFC *see:* Goats

Llandudno Swifts FC (Swifts) *see also:*
  Canaries

Llandybïe / Llandebie United FC
  (Limemen)

Llandybïe RFC (Tybïe)

Llandyrnog United FC (Dyrny)

Llandysul FC (Babes, Swallows)

Llanedeyrn Bulldogs FC (Bulldogs)

Mid-Rhondda FC (Mushrooms / Mush)

Milford Haven RFC (Mariners)

Milford United FC (Robins, United)

Mochdre Dragons DFC (Dragons)

Mochdre Lions DFC (Lions)

Mold Alexandra FC (Alex)

Monkton Swifts FC (Swifts)

Monmouth RFC (Druids)

Monmouth Town FC (Kingfishers)

Monmouthshire Police RFC (Bobbies)

Montgomery Town FC (Canaries)

Montgomeryshire Marauders RLFC (Marauders)

Morriston Olympic FC (Olympic, Rads)

Moscow Dynamo FC (Dynamos)

Mostyn Dragons FC (Dragons)

Motherwell FC (Steelmen)

Mountain Ash RFC (Mount, Old Firm)

Mumbles RFC (Seasiders)

Nant Conwy CR / RFC (Teirw Nant Conwy)

Nantlle Vale CPD / FC (Vale)

Nantyffyllon RFC (Nanty, Reds)

Nant-y-moel RFC *see:* White Stars

Nant-y-moel White Stars FC (White Stars)

Narberth FC (Bluebirds)

Narberth RFC [Pennsylvania] (Otters)

Narberth RFC [Pennsylvania] (Otters)

Natal Sharks RFC (Sharks)

Neath Allied Traders RFC (Shoppies / Shoppoes)

Neath FC (Eagles)

Neath Port Talbot Steelers RLFC (Steelers)

Neath RFC (All Blacks, Mourners) *see also:* Ospreys, Scorpions

Nefyn United FC (Penwaig)

Nelson Cavaliers FC (Cavaliers / Cavs)

Nelson RFC (Unicorns)

New Dock Stars RFC (Stars)

New Quay FC (Mackerel Men, Quays, Seasiders)

New Saints, The FC [Y Seintiau Newydd] (Saints)

New Tredegar RFC (Newts, Silverbacks)

New Zealand, *national rugby team* (All Blacks)

Newbridge RFC (Bridge)

Newbridge-on-Wye FC (Bridgemen, Wyesiders)

Newcastle AFC (Millers)

Newcastle Emlyn FC (Reds)

Newcastle Emlyn RFC (Red & Whites)

Newcastle Falcons RFC (Falcons)

Newcastle United FC (Magpies, United)

Newport AFC (Ironsides)

Newport Civil Service FC (Civil)

Newport County FC (Exiles; Ironsides) *see also:* Black & Ambers

Newport Gwent Dragons RFC (Dragons)

Newport RFC (Black &Ambers, Usksiders)

Newport Saracens RFC (Saracens / Sarries)

Newport Strikers LFC (Strikers)

Newport Titans RLFC (Titans) *see also:* Rhinos

Newry City FC (Bordermen)

Newton Wanderers FC (Wanderers)

Newtown Excelsior FC (Excelsior)

Newtown FC (Batmans, Robins) *see also:* Amateurs, Stars

Newtown White Stars FC (Stars)

Neyland FC (Nomads)

Port Talbot Blue Stars FC (Blue Stars)

Port Talbot FC (Blues, Steelmen)

Port Talbot Tigers FC (Tigers)

Port Tennant Colts FC (Colts)

Porth, AFC (Black Dragons)

Porth Harlequins RFC (Quins)

Porth Tywyn Suburbs FC (Suburbs)

Porth-cawl FC (Seasiders)

Porth-cawl RFC (Seasiders, Seaweeds)
see also: Blue Bulls

Porthmadog CPD / FC (Madocians / Madocites, Port)

Prendergast Villa FC (Villa / Villans)

Preseli Warriors DFC (Warriors)

Prestatyn & Rhyl Panthers RLFC (Panthers)

Prestatyn Town FC (Campers, Seasiders)

Presteigne St. Andrews FC (Saints)

Preston North End FC (Lilywhites, North End)

Prysor Rovers FC (Traws)

Pyle RFC (Blue & Whites, Scrumpies)

Queen of the South FC see: Ravers

Rangers FC (Rangers) *see also:* Old Firm

Raith Rovers FC (Rovers) *see also:* Ravers

Reading FC (Royals)

RGC 1404 RFC (Gogs)

Rhayader Town FC (Red Kites, Thin Red Line)

Rhiwbina RFC (Squirells)

Rhondda, AFC (Black Dragons)

Rhos Aelwyd FC (Aelwyd)

Rhos-goch Rangers FC (Crows)

Rhuddlan Town FC (Castlemen)

Rhuthun *see:* Ruthin

Rhydyfelin RFC (Village / Villagers)

Rhyl Coasters RLFC (Coasters)

Rhyl Exiles RLFC (Exiles)

Rhyl FC (Beavers, Lilywhites) *see also:* Hearts

Rhyl Hearts FC (Hearts)

Rhyl Skull & Crossbones FC (Skull & Crossbones)

Rhymney RFC (Brewers)

Risca RFC (Cuckoos)

Risca Town FC (Cuckoos)

Roath Ravers FC (Ravers)

Roath RFC (Zebras)

Rogerstone FC (Rogie Aces)

Rogerstone RFC (Rogie)

Rotherham United FC (Millers)

Royal Regiment of Wales XV (Royals)

RTB Ebbw Vale RFC (Green & Whites)

Rumney RFC (Rhinos)

Rumney Rhinos RLFC (Rhinos) *see also:* Titans

Ruthin CR / RFC (Blues)

Ruthin Town FC (Blues, Ruthinites, Ruthless, Ruths)

Rwanda, *national rugby team* (Silverbacks)

St. Alban's RFC ('Buns)

St. Asaph City FC (Saints)

St. Clair's FC (Saints)

St. Clears FC (Saints)

St. David's RFC (Saints)

St. Dogmael's FC (Saints)

St. Florence FC (Saints)

St. Harmon & District FC (Swifts)

St. Ishmael's FC (Tish)

St. Joseph's FC (Saints)

St. Joseph's Old Boys RFC (Saints)

St. Joseph's RFC (Joe's)

St. Mellon's, Trowbridge & Rumney RFC *see:* STAR RFC

St. Paul's RFC (Irishmen)

Tottenham Hotspur FC (Hotspur)

Trallwm FC (Tigers)

Trawsfynydd FC (Traws)

Traws-goed FC (Traws)

Trebanos RFC (Ancient Borough, 'Banws). *see also:* Rooks

Tredegar Ironsides RFC (Irons)

Tredomen FC (Engineers)

Trefechan FC (Turks)

Trefeurig & District United FC (Canaries)

Trefonen FC (Pitmen, Yellows)

Trefor (Trevor) Comrades FC (Comrades)

Tregaron CR / RFC (Teirw Duon)

Tregaron Turfs FC (Turfs)

Treharris Athletic Western FC (Lilywhites, Western)

Treharris FC (All Whites, Lilywhites)

Treharris Phoenix RFC (Phoenix)

Treharris RFC *see:* Phoenix

Treherbert RFC (Devils)

Treherbert Shoppies RFC (Shoppies)

Treorchy RFC (Blues, Orkeis / Orkyites, Royals, Zebras)

Treowen Stars FC (Stars)

Trethomas Bluebirds FC (Bluebirds)

Trevor Comrades FC (Comrades)

Trinant RFC (Troggs)

Trinity St. David's University RFC (Fighting Parsons, Mad Pilgrims, Old Parsonians)

Troedyrhiw Stars FC (Stars)

Tumble RFC (Magpies)

Tŷ-croes RFC (All Blacks)

Tydfil Wildcats RLFC (Wildcats)

Tylorstown RFC (Scarlets, Tigers)

Tynte Rovers FC (Rovers)

Tywyn / Bryn-crug FC (Cormorants)

Undy Athletic FC *see:* Limemen

Unedig Pen-y-bryn FC (United)

UWIC Cardiff FC *see:* Cardiff Metropolitan FC

UWIC Cardiff RFC *see:* Cardiff Metroplitan RFC

UWIC Inter Cardiff FC (Div's, International, Sheep) *see also:* Seagulls

Valley Cougars RLFC (Cougars)

Vardre RFC (Magpies)

Venture Community FC (Venga Boys)

Vista FC (Bulldogs)

Wales, *national football team* (Crysau Cochion, Dragons, Red Devils, Red Dragons, Young Dragons)

Wales, *national rugby team* (Crysau Cochion, Dragons, Red Dragons, Young Dragons)

Wanderers FC (Wanderers)

Wasps RFC *see:* London Wasps RFC

Waterloo Rovers FC (Rovers)

Watford FC (Hornets)

Wattstown RFC (Ducks, Terriers)

Waunarlwydd RFC (Green & Blacks, Waun)

Waunfawr FC (Beganifs)

Welsh Academicals XV RFC (Accies)

Welshpool RFC ('Pool)

Welshpool Town FC (Lilywhites, 'Pool)

Wenvoe Exiles FC (Exiles)

West Bromwich Albion FC (Albion/s)

West Dragons FC (Dragons)

West End FC (Swansea Wellingtons) *see also:* United

West End United FC (United)

West Ham United FC *see:* Clarets

West Wales Sharks RLFC (Sharks)

West Wales Wild Boars RLFC (Wild Boars)

INDEX TO PERSONAL AND CORPORATE NAMES

Bowes, James, *of Cardiff* (Scorpions)

Boyce, Max, *singer* (Pooler)

Brecon, *Lordship of* (Raiders)

British Glanzstoff Manufacturing Company, Flint (Silkmen)

British Nylon Spinners, Pontypool (Spinners)

British Steel (SCOWS)

Brychan Brycheiniog (Martyrs, Royals, Tybïe)

Brynkinallt Colliery, Chirk (Colliers)

BSA, *motorcycles* (Barracudas)

Cadoxton Conservative Club (Imps)

Caereinion High School, Powys (COBRAS)

Calsonic Kansei Corporation, Llanelli (Radicals)

Cambridge University (Blue & Blacks)

Cardiff Metropolitan University (Archers)

Cardiff University (Academicals /Accies)

Cennych (Cennech), *Saint* (Cennech)

Cenydd, *Saint* (Saints)

Cogan Coronation Club, Penarth (Coronation)

Comrades of the Great War (Comrades)

Cornwell, David (1841–1906), *of Penarth* (Donkey Island Butcher Boys)

Courtaulds, Flint (Silkmen)

Cravos, Sydney, *of Cardiff* (Rags / Rags & Tatters)

Crayston, Jack (1910–92) (Dazzlers)

Culwch ('Twrch)

Cyril the Swan, *mascot* (Swans)

Charles I (1600–49), *King* (Cavaliers)

Darren Colliery, Trebanos ('Banws)

David, *Saint* (Royals, Saints)

Davies, D. L., *of Aberystwyth* (Black & Green)

Davies, Dai, *international goalkeeper* (Stars)

Davies, Ogwyn, *of Tregaron* (Teirw Duon)

Davis, Joe, *of Cemaes Bay FC* (Demolition Squad)

De Bohun Family, *of Caldicot* (Swans)

De Monhault, Roger (Bucks)

De Winton & Co., *of Caernarfon* ('Nops)

Democritus, *Greek philosopher* (Laughing Philosophers)

Dinamo Sports and Fitness Club, Moscow (Dynamos)

Dinorwig Slate Quarry, Llanberis (Tigers)

Dolgellau County School (Hen Ramadegwyr)

Downie's, Messrs, *of Aberystwyth* (Black & Green)

Écoles Normale (Normalites)

Edward, *Black Prince* (Black Army)

Edwards, Huntley (Darans)

Emlyn Colliery, Pen-y-groes (Colliers)

Evans & Williams, *wagon works at Llanelli* (Albies)

Evans Bevan Family, *of Neath* (Black & Tans, Evans Bevan Boys, Seven)

Evans, Albert (1902–68), *of Llanelli* (Albies)

Evans, Ellis Humphrey (Hedd Wyn; 1897–1917) (Flower)

Evans, Peter, *of Penarth* (Coronation)

Evans, Trevor, *rugby international* (Amman)

Ferodo, *factory at Caernarfon* (Brake Linings)

Ffraid, *Saint* (Saints)

Martin, Gary, *of Dafen Welfare FC*
(Blues)

Merlin (Wizards)

Merrett, Herbert, *of Cardiff City FC*
(Red Devils)

Midland Bank (Griffins)

Miners' Welfare Institutes (Welfare)

Monkton House School, Cardiff
(Wanderers)

Morgan, Walter, *of Pontypridd*
(Butchers' Arms Boys)

Moxham, E. C., *of Neath* (All Blacks)

Mumford, Simon (Accies)

National Coal Board (Engineers)

National Docks Labour Board
(Dockers)

National Eisteddfod of Wales, 1917,
Birkenhead (Flower)

Nelson, Horatio (1758–1805), *Viscount*
(Cavaliers)

Northgate Brewery, Connah's Quay
(Westenders)

Ogden, Thomas, *of Bolton* (Wanderers)

Ogmore, *Lordship of* (Raiders)

Old Stager, *pseud.* (Old Firm)

Olympic Radiators, Carmarthen
(Rads)

Olwen *see:* Twrch

Orielton School (Seagulls)

Owain Glyndŵr (c. 1354–1416),
Prince of Wales (Gogs)

Owen, Iolo, *of Glantraeth* (Glan)

Parry, Owen (Now), *of Llanfairpwll*
(Super Reds)

Peel, *Sir* Robert (1788–1850)
(Bobbies)

Penson, Richard Kyrke (1816–86),
architect (Limemen)

Percy, *Sir* Henry, 'Harry Hotspur'
(Hotspur)

Peris, *Saint* (Berries)

Pontyfelin Institute for Leisure,
Culture & Sport (PILCS)

Powell Duffryn Co. (Engineers)

Powell, W. R. H. MP (1819–89), *of*
Llanboidy (Foxes)

Pryse Family, *of Gogerddan* (Lions,
Roosters)

Race, Roy (Roy of the Rovers)
(Rovers)

Rees, Thomas Williams, *of Cardiff*
(Blue & Blacks)

Rhondda Borough Council (Black
Dragons)

Rhosite, *pseud., poet* (Classics)

Rhymney Breweries Ltd. (Brewers)

Riverboat Club, Caerau (Riverboaters)

Riverside Golf Range, Aberdulais
(Dingle Boys)

Roberts, Bruce, *of Killay FC* (Clarets)

Robinson, Ted, *of Wrexham FC*
(Robins)

Rocky the Robin, *mascot* (Robins)

Rogers, Thomas Langdon (1877–
1966), *of Swansea* (Brotherhood)

Rolling Stones, *pop group* (Roosters)

Romilly, John (1802–74) *1st Baron*
Romilly of Barry, (Laughing
Philosophers)

Roy of the Rovers (Roy Race) (Rovers)

Royal Aircraft Establishment, Aber-
porth (Airmen, Rockets)

Royal Artillery (Gunners)

Royal Irish Police (Black & Tans)

Royal Leicestershire Regiment (Tigers)

Saladin (Saracens / Sarries)

Sami Seagull, *mascot* (Seagulls)

Siemens, Ernst Werner von (1816–
1892) (Dynamos)

Smith, Owen, *member of Parliament*

BIBLIOGRAPHY

Abbott, R.: 'Chronicles of a Caernarvon ironworks'. *Transactions of the Caernarfonshire Historical Society*, 17 (1956), 86–94.

Aberaman Rugby Union Football Club: centenary 1890–1990. (1990).

Aberystwyth RFC, 1947–1997: 50th anniversary. (1997).

Alexander, David: *Stars on a Saturday afternoon: the story of Crynant RFC*. (1991).

Ambrosen, A. K.: *Amber in the blood: a history of Newport County*. (1993).

Appleton, Meirion: *Appy: Bont, busnes a byd y bêl*. (2011)

Barrett, Clive: *100 years of Spa football, 1883–1983*: [Llandrindod Wells]. (1983).

Bevan, Kenny: *Bois y Llan: Llangennech RFC (1885–1985)*. (1987).

Boulton, William G.: *Senghenydd: the village and its rugby club*. (1982).

Brookes, Allan: *A club for all seasons: Kenfig Hill FC*. (2005).

Cadwallader, T. Graham: *Record: history of rugby clubs in the Amman, Dulais and Swansea Valleys*. (1966).

Carmarthen Rugby Football Club: centenary year, 1874–1974. (1974)

The centenary history of Amman United Rugby Football Club, 1903–2003. (2003)

Charles, B. G.: *The place-names of Pembrokeshire*. (1992).

Clwb Rygbi Bethesda, 1974–1984. (1984).

Clwb Rygbi Bro Ffestiniog: 1973–1994. (1994).

Clwb Rygbi Caernarfon: y deng mlynedd ar hugain cyntaf. (2003).

The Colourful history of the Lilywhites:[Rhyl AFC]. (1989).

Crooks, John: *Cardiff City Football Club: the official history of the Bluebirds*. (1992).

Daniel, Raymond & Olwen Daniel: *Llyfr mawr Llanddewi Brefi*. (2011).

David, John: *Hard kicks but good touches!: a celebration of 100 years of rugby at Pontyclun*. (1987).

Davies, Dai: *Hanner cystal â 'Nhad: hunangofiant gôlgeidwad rhyngwladol*. (1983)

Davies, Daniel E.: *Cardiff Rugby Club: history and statistics 1876–1975*. (1976).

Davies, David Wyn: *The Maglonians: one hundred years of football in Machynlleth (1885–1985)*. (1985).

Davies, Elwyn (editor): *Rhestr o enwau lleoedd / A gazetteer of Welsh place-names*. (1967).

Davies, Gareth M.: *A coast of soccer memories, 1894–1994: the centenary book of the North Wales Coast Football Association*. (1994).

Davies, Gareth M. & Ian Garland: *Who's who of Welsh international soccer players*. (1991).

Davies, Keith: *125 years of rugby, 1875–2000: Abergavenny Rugby Football Club*.

(2001).

Davies, Ken: 'Newtown's senior cup finals'. *The Newtonian*, 49 (2012), 25–31.

Davies, Lynn: *Geirfa'r glöwr*. (1976).

Davies, R. Gwynn: *Y Waun a'i phobl*. (1996).

Davies, T. E.: *Tŷcroes Rugby Football Club*. (1979).

Davies, Vernon: *Treorchy Rugby Football Club, 1886–1986*. (1986).

Davis, Jack: *Newport Rugby Football Club, 1875–1960*. (1960).

Evans & Williams Sports FC: *Fiftieth anniversary celebration dinner ... official souvenir programme*. (2010)

Evans, Barbara M.: *Blaina Rugby Football Club, 1875–1976: memories of Mutton Tump*. (1976).

Evans, C. J. O.: *Glamorgan: its history and topography*. (1953).

Evans, C. J. O.: *Monmouthshire: its history and topography*. (1954).

Evans, Chris: *The industrial and social history of Seven Sisters*. (1964).

Evans, Gareth & Stan Morton: *Hanes Clwb Rygbi Rhuthun, / a history of Ruthin Rugby Club*, translated by Hafina Clwyd. (2011).

Farmer, David: *The life and times of Swansea RFC: the All Whites*. (1995).

Fisher, Paul: *100 years of Port Talbot Football Club: celebrating 1901–2001*. (2001).

Fowler, Brian: *Ammanford RFC centenary, 1887–1987*. [1987].

Francis, Hywel: *Magnificent Seven, 1897–1997: the centenary history of Seven Sisters Rugby Club*, (1997).

Garland, Ian: *The history of the Welsh Cup, 1877–1993*. (1993).

Garland, Ian & Wyn Gray-Thomas: *The Canaries sing again: a history of Caernarfon Town Football Club*. (1986).

Geiriadur Prifysgol Cymru / A Dictionary of the Welsh language. (1950–).

Grey-Williams, Dilwyn: 'Unlocking the mystery of the Beganifs'. *Gwreiddiau Gwynedd Roots*, 2 / 59 (2010), 12–14.

The Gwent village book, compiled by the Gwent Federation of Women's Institutes from notes and illustrations sent by Institutes in the County. (1994).

Harragan, Bob: *Llanelli Rugby Club*. (1998).

Harris, Gareth & Alan Evans: *The Butchers' Arms Boys*. [Pontypridd RFC]. (1997).

Harris, Johnathan: 'Association football in Breconshire, 1900–1929'. *Brycheiniog*, 29 (1996/97), 105–11.

Hitchings, Winifred M.: *Seagull Billy*. (1929).

Hopkins, Bleddyn: *Swansea RFC*. (2002).

Howell, Jenkin (1836–1902): 'Dyffryn Cynon'. *Y Geninen*, 1900, pp. 268–9; 1903, pp. 141–2.

Hughes, Alan: *Tonna RFC: its village and its rugby club*. (2012).

Hughes, Gareth: *The Scarlets: a history of Llanelli Rugby Football Club*. (1986).

Humphreys, Gwilym E.: *Heyrn yn y tân: atgofion addysgwr*. (2000).

Hussell, Alan: *A concise history of Aberavon RFC*. (1990).

Huws, Richard E.: *Caneris melyn Trefeurig / Trefeurig's yellow canaries*. (2010).

Huws, Richard E.: *The football and rugby playing fields of Wales*. (2009).

Huws, Richard E.: *The footballers of Borth and Ynys-las, 1873–1950*. (2011).

Jefferies, Horace: *100 years in black and white*. [Cross Keys RFC]. (1985).

Jenkins, David R. & David Lloyd: *Magic, sheer bloody magic: Nantyffyllon RFC*. (2002).

Jenkins, Elwyn: *Pwll, pêl a phulpud*. (2008).

Jenkins, Geraint: *Yr Elyrch: dathlu'r 100*. (2012).

Jenkins, Geraint: *Proud to be a Swan: the history of Swansea City AFC, 1912–2012*. (2012).

Jenkins, Gwyn: *The history of the Aberystwyth & District Football League, 1934–84*. (1984).

Jenkins, Jabez Edmund (1840–1903): *Vaynor, its history and guide*. (1879).

Jenkins, John M, Duncan Pierce & Timothy Auty: *Who's who of Welsh international rugby players* (1991).

Johnes, Martin: *Soccer and society: south Wales, 1900–1939*. (2002).

Johnes, Martin & Ian Garland: " 'The new craze': football and society in north-east Wales." *Welsh History Review*, 22/2 (2004), 278–304.

Jones, Andrew S.: *Tonna Rugby Football Club: centenary year*. (1987).

Jones, Arwel: *Y Darans: clwb pêl-droed Llanberis*. (1991).

Jones, D. Mansel: *Canmlwyddiant / Centenary Ystradgynlais RFC*. (1992).

Jones, Gwynfor Pierce: *De Winton of Caernarfon: engineers of excellence*. (2011).

Jones, Howard M.: *Yr Hendy: the village and rugby club*. (1993).

Jones, J. R.: *The history of Pontardawe RFC*. (1985).

Jones, Ken: *Hanes hanner can mlynedd Clwb Pêl Droed y Bont*. (1997).

Jones, Vernon A.: *The Turfs: a brief history of Tregaron Football Club*. (1994).

Joseph, Clive: *Baglan RFC 1962–2012: celebrating 50 years of rugby*. (2012).

Lampeter Town Rugby Football Club Centenary Year Brochure. (1979).

Lawrie, W. A. D.: *The history of Bridgend Rugby Football Club: the first 100 years*. (1980).

Lewis, Gerrard: *Between the lines*: [memoirs of a FIFA referee]. (2007). subtitle added

Lewis, Siân: *Rhys and the cuckoo of Risca*. (1997).

Lewis, Steve: *Newport Rugby Football Club, 1974–1950*. (1999).

Lewis, Tony: *A history of Kenfig Hill RFC*. (1973).

Lile, Brian & David Farmer: 'The early development of association football in South Wales, 1890–1906'. *Transactions of the Honourable Society of Cymmrodorion* (1984), 193–215.

Lush, Peter & Dave Farrar (editors): *Tries in the valleys: a history of rugby league in Wales*. (1998)

Lloyd, Lewis: *De Winton of Caernarfon, 1854–1892*. (1994).

McInery, Jeff: *The Linnets – an illustrated, narrative history of Barry Town AFC, 1888–1993*. (1994).

Mathews, John E.: *From pit to pitch: a pictorial history of football in Rhos*. (c.1991).

Minutes and Yearbook of the Methodist Conference. (1966).

Mole, Robert: *Whatever happened to the Tugboatonians?: a history of the Newport & District Football League*. (2002).

Morgan, Terry: *Tŷcroes RFC 75th Anniversary Programme: 1911–86*. (1986).

Moses, Anthony J.: *A history of Dinas Powys Rugby Football Club*. (1982).

Musselwhite, John W.: *The Butcher Boys of Donkey Island* [Penarth RFC]. (1980).

100 years of rugby and village life at Llandybïe: 1901–2001. (2001).

Owen, Andrew: *Come on the Bay: Colwyn Bay Football Club 125th anniversary*. (2005).

Owen, Denley: *Powell Maesgwynne: philanthropist, sporting great and radical hero*. (2012).

Owen, Gwilym: *Crych dros dro*. (2003).

Owen, Gwyn Pierce: *C'mon reff!* (1999).

Owen, Hywel Wyn & Richard Morgan: *Dictionary of the place-names of Wales*. (2007).

Parry, Peter, Brian Lile & Donald Griffiths: *The Old Black and Green*. [Aberystwyth FC]. (1987).

Pembroke Dock Harlequins Rugby Football Club: 1880–1980. (c. 1981).

Powell, Terry: *An illustrated history of Newbridge RFC*. (1988).

Preece, Tony & Charles Huskings: *Abercarn Rugby Football Club: centenary souvenir book*. (1995).

Prescott, Gwyn: *"The best and happiest team"* [Cardiff HSOB Rugby]. (1978).

Prescott, Gwyn: *"This rugby spellbound people": rugby football in nineteenth-century Cardiff and south Wales* (Cardiff, 2011).

Price, Mike: *Neath Athletic: 50 years of rugby*. (1997).

Rees, D. Ben: *Hanes plwyf Llanddewi Brefi*. (1984).

Rees, E. A.: *Welsh outlaws and bandits: political rebellion and lawlessness in Wales, 1400–1603*. (2001).

Rees, J. Hywel: *The Gowerton Rugby Football Club, 1884–1984: one hundred years on*. (1984).

Rees, Rod: *Tunnel o rygbi: hanes clwb rygbi Cwmtwrch, 1890–1990 / a ton of rugby: the history of Cwmtwrch RFC, 1890–1990*. (1990).

Roberts, Nigel: *The history of Chirk Football Club, 1876–2002*. (2003).

Robinson, John: *The supporters' guide to Welsh football ...* (1994–).

Ruddick, Ray: *Pontypool Rugby Football Club.* (2002).

Shepherd, Richard: *Cardiff City Football Club, 1899–1947.* (1996).

Smith, David & Gareth Williams: *Fields of praise: the official history of the Welsh Rugby Union.* (1980).

Stead, Phil: *Red Dragons: the story of Welsh football.* (2012).

Stennett, Ceri: *As good as it gets: the centenary book of the Welsh Schools Football Association 1911–2011.* (2011).

Sweet, Philip: *Merthyr Town AFC, 1908–1934: a history.* (2007).

Tremlett, George: *Laugharne RFC 1893–1993: centenary booklet,* (1993).

Twydell, Dave: *'Rejected FC': comprehensive histories of ex-Football League clubs. Volume 1.* (1988). Aberdare Athletic, pp. 7–28.

Thau, Chris: *The spirit of Penarth: one hundred and thirty-one years of seaside rugby: 1880–2001.* (2011).

Thau, Chris: *Tonmawr RFC, 1887–1997: a century of passion.* (1997).

Thomas, Cyril D.: *Swansea Senior Football League: 1901–2001, 100 years of local soccer.* (2002).

Thomas, David Peter: *A view from the Garth: one hundred years of Taff's Well rugby, 1887–1987.* (1987).

Thomas, Eric: *Canmlwyddiant Clwb Rygbi Brynaman.* (1998).

Tyas, Shaun: *The dictionary of football club nicknames in Britain and Ireland.* (2013, forthcoming).

Walters, Philip M.: 'Rugby football at Aberdare', [in] *Old Aberdare,* Vol. 3 (1984), pp. 29–55.

Watkins, David: *Merthyr Tydfil Football Club; memories of Penydarren Park.* (2006).

Welsh Football: the national football magazine of Wales, (1992–).

Welsh Rugby (originally *Rugger Sport*), 1961–83.

Westcott, Gordon: *A century on the rugby beat: a history of 100 years of police rugby football in the South Wales Constabulary area.* (1992).

Williams, Alan: *100 years of Mumbles rugby, 1887–1987.* (1987)

Williams. Orig: *Cario'r Ddraig: stori El Bandito.* (1985).

Wmffre, Iwan: *The place-names of Cardiganshire.* (2004).